ORIGIN

OF THE

SIKH POWER IN THE PUNJAB,

AND

POLITICAL LIFE OF

MUHA-RAJA RANJEET SINGH

ORIGIN

OF THE

SIKH POWER IN THE PUNJAB

AND

POLITICAL LIFE OF

MUHA-RAJA RANJEET SINGH

WITH AN ACCOUNT OF THE PRESENT CONDITION, RELIGION, LAWS AND CUSTOMS OF SIKHS.

COMPILED BY

HENRY T. PRINSEP

GYAN

Published by

Gyan Publishing House
5, Ansari Road
Daryaganj, New Delhi-110002
Phone: 011-47034999, 9811692060
E-mail: books@gyanbooks.com

Distribution Network
gyanbooks.com
India, USA, Canada, UK, Australia, France

ISBN: 978-81-212-9092-0-(PB)
First Published, 1834

2nd Impression 2023

Printed at: Gyan Press, Delhi.

ORIGIN OF THE SIKH POWER IN THE PUNJAB, AND POLITICAL LIFE OF MUHA-RAJA RANJEET SINGH

COMPILER: HENRY T. PRINSEP

MUHARAJA RUNJEET SINGH

from a portrait by Jewun Ram a native
artist of Delhi, who accompanied the Governor General
to the interview at Roopur in 1831

Kasnath sculpsit

ORIGIN

OF THE

SIKH POWER IN THE PUNJAB,

AND

POLITICAL LIFE OF

MUHA-RAJA RUNJEET SINGH,

WITH AN ACCOUNT OF THE PRESENT CONDITION,
RELIGION, LAWS AND CUSTOMS OF THE SIKHS.

COMPILED BY

HENRY T. PRINSEP,

OF THE BENGAL CIVIL SERVICE,

FROM A REPORT BY CAPTAIN WILLIAM MURRAY, LATE POLITICAL
AGENT AT UMBALA, AND FROM OTHER SOURCES.

CALCUTTA:

G. H. HUTTMANN, MILITARY ORPHAN PRESS.

1834.

PREFACE.

THERE is an interest attaching to the character and fortunes of RUNJEET SINGH, and to the dominion he has established over the Punjab and the Sikh nation, which promises to ensure to the following pages a favorable reception from the British Public. This interest is founded not less upon the geographical position of the territory of the new state, than upon the fact of its having been silently growing up under our eyes, till our wonder is excited at the accumulation of power and of wealth at the command of its present head. The desire to learn the steps and the means, by which the founder of any empire has risen to greatness, is a natural curiosity of the human mind, intense in proportion to the exaltation reached: but in this instance there is proximity to our own possessions, with the collisions that have occurred in consequence, to add to the interest felt about

RUNJEET SINGH; besides that the tract of country, now forming the Sikh kingdom, is in the high road by which every conqueror from the west has penetrated into Hindoostan; and speculation is always more or less afloat, as to the possibility of a similar conquest being again attempted, by the armies of Europe associated, or by those of the Northern Autocrat alone, whose views of aggrandizement seem insatiable, and have long been directed towards Persia and the East.

The time thus appears to be favorable for an attempt to offer to the Public some information as to the present condition of the Punjab and its Ruler: and every one must have felt, that there is a blank in the intelligence possessed on this subject, not consistent with the general state of knowledge, or the eagerness with which information, and in particular political and statistical information, is in these days poured forth upon the Public, by every one who thinks he has any thing to communicate, that will be listened to or received. The early history of the Sikhs is pretty generally known: few are ignorant, that they are a religious sect, established in the time of BABUR by NANUK SHAH, the propagator of doctrines of universal toleration, and the zealous projector of an union of faith between the Hindoos and Mahommedans, on the basis of the unity of the Godhead. In like manner it would be superfluous to recapitulate in a work like this, how the sect was continued, and its tenets and creed embodied in sacred volumes called Grunths, by a succession of ten sainted Gooroos, ending with Gooroo Govind, who lived in the time of Aurungzeeb, and who, meeting persecution, converted his followers from peaceable and industrious citizens, into deadly enemies to the Moghul empire and Mooslim faith. All this has been fully traced and explained in various publications: so also the vain attempts of Banda, and other Martyrs who followed Gooroo Govind, against the too great strength of the Dehlee sovereignty and its officers, under the immediate successors of Aurungzeeb: but the rise of the sect, from the dust into which it seemed to be beaten down by persecution, to its present splendour of exaltation, has not hitherto been made the subject of any one's investigation and research; and the matter consequently comprised in this volume is given confidently as new, and as not to be found elsewhere. It is our duty and our present object to explain where and how it has been obtained.

The British Government has since 1808 been the protector of the Sikh territory lying between the Sutlej and Jumna: Its officers have been appealed to for the adjustment of all disputes between the chiefs and their neighbours or dependants, and the references to the Supreme Council of Government at the Presidency are frequent, and involve questions of great intricacy, making the management of our relations in that quarter by no means the least troublesome part of the business submitted to its decision. Lord WILLIAM BENTINCK was led by the perception of this circumstance to seek from the officers employed in the management of Sikh affairs, some general information as to the history and condition of the chiefs, and the habits and customs of the sect. Accordingly, when preparing for his journey to Hindoostan, in 1830, he called upon Captain MURRAY, the Political Agent at Umbala, who had for more than fifteen years been employed in conducting our relations with the Sikh chiefs on the British side of the Sutlej, for a report upon the subject. Captain WADE, the Assistant at Loodeeana, who had latterly been entrusted with the subordinate charge, under the Resident at Dehlee, of the correspondence with RUNJEET SINGH, was similarly called upon, and both officers submitted voluminous reports, containing valuable information on all the points required. That of Captain MURRAY seemed to be the result of much reading and research, and to be prepared from materials collected during the whole period of his residence amongst the Sikhs. He had evidently consulted with care all the Persian and other books, that afford any insight into the history of the Sikhs, or of the Moghul and Afghan officers who came into contact or collision with them; while his account of the rise and fortunes of RUNJEET SINGH appeared to have been compiled from the reports and verbal information of intelligent persons who had served under him, corrected and tested by a laborious examination of the Akhbars or native newspapers, files of which were recorded in his office: a valuable Appendix was added, containing the result of his personal observations and enquiries into the habits, customs, rules, and observances of the Sikhs. The report was defective in arrangement, being put together with no view to publication, but unfortunately this highly esteemed and distinguished officer died very soon after the Governor General visited those parts, when it was his Lordship's intention to have requested him to prepare from his expose, a volume calculated to diffuse the information he had collected, and to give public and general utility to the result of his labours.

There is no doubt, that, if this officer had lived, the work would have been executed in a manner worthy of his abilities. His sudden death has rendered it necessary, that what he left incomplete, and had put together in haste, without due order, or arrangement, or regard to the accuracies of style, should be completed and revised by another hand. The whole of the historical part of his report has required to be re-written: The arrangement has been partially altered, and the narrative has been cast into chapters in the form it now assumes, besides which there is new matter added from Captain WADE's report and from other sources. It has hence been impossible to place Captain MURRAY's name on the title-page as the author, so as to make him responsible, before the public, for what he never saw or approved. It will however be understood that, except in the tenth and eleventh Chapters of Continuation, the task of the Compiler of the following pages has been merely that of *redacteur*, and that the merit of having collected the information, which gives to the work any interest or value it may possess, belongs almost entirely to Captain MURRAY. Indeed, next to the desire to rescue from the oblivion of a record-office, information calculated to be so extensively useful, and to give to the Public, access to what had been collected with so much labour and research, the motive that has principally influenced the Compiler to undertake the preparation of this volume for the press, has been the wish to do honor to this distinguished and lamented officer, and to lay before his friends, and the world, a lasting testimony of his worth and talents.

The task has been performed during the leisure of a sea voyage and residence in Van Diemen's Land for health. Nothing has since been added, and the narrative accordingly terminates abruptly with the Treaties concluded by the British Government with Sindh in 1832. It would doubtless have cost little additional trouble to have introduced another chapter bringing down the course of events to the present day (1834;) but to do so would have required a resort to records, and to documents not legitimately within the Compiler's reach, or familiar to his recollection, and from their connection with passing transactions, not ripe probably for public exhibition. To such, therefore, he has not sought access, and after all, until the career of the Ruler of the Punjab shall have reach- its natural term, the close of the narrative must have been equally abrupt, wheresoever the line had been drawn. It has hence appeared preferable to let the curtain drop for the present, at the marked epoch of the conclusion of the Treaties referred to, which were published in the past year, reserving what may follow, to the date of the decease of the prominent character of the work, to be added hereafter, in case at any future period the public should take sufficient interest in the affairs of the Punjab, to call for a renewed publication.

It may be proper to add, that while the first part of this work was already in the Printer's hands, a Persian account of the affairs of the Sikhs in the Punjab, was obligingly communicated to the Compiler by Sir CHARLES METCALFE. The manuscript had been delivered to Sir CHARLES by its author, KHOOSHWUQT RAEE, who was for many years the Agent and Intelligencer of the British Government at Umritsur. The narrative comes down to 1812 only, but is very full in respect to the early history of the Sikh Sirdars, and contains much information and useful matter, not to be found elsewhere. The opportunity which was thus presented of comparing an original work of this kind with the Memoir of Captain MURRAY, has not been lost. The result has afforded a satisfactory corroboration of the accuracy of this officer: indeed, the correspondence of date and circumstance in many important particulars leads almost to the conclusion, that KHOOSHWUQT RAEE's narrative must have been amongst the materials from which the Memoir was prepared. Some occasional discrepancies and additional facts or illustrations have been noted separately at the close of the volume. The Compiler's grateful acknowledgments are particularly due to Sir CHARLES METCALFE, for the liberal frankness with which so valuable a material has been made available to improve and correct this publication, and it is to the same high quarter, that he is indebted for access to the materials from which the Map has been constructed, which is prefixed to the volume.

H. T. P.

Calcutta, May, 1834.

ERRATA.

PAGE

2—last line, for "*Pakul*" read *Pahul*.

6—second line, for "*gusool*" read *yusoul*.

18—last line but one, for "HULKOR" read HOLKUR.

19—date in the heading, for "1769" read 1760.

22—nineteenth line, for "*Pakul*" read *Pahul*.

23—eighth line, for "*raise*" read *raze*.

24—sixteenth line, for "*Baroach*" read *Baraich*.

26—twenty-first line, for "*the Governor and Zyn Khan*" read *the Governor Zyn Khan*.

29—fifteenth line, for "*Jhundee Singh*" read *Jhunda Singh*.

30—first line, for "*Nukreea Misul*" read *Nukeea Misul*.

30—second line, for "*Nukree*" read *Nukee*.

39—seventh and seventeenth lines, for "*Busuntee*" read *Busuntur*.

45—eleventh and seventh lines from the bottom, for "*Battala*" read *Butala*.

47—tenth line from the bottom, for "*Soodhurp*" read *Soohdura*.

61—twelfth line, for "*Deenanugur*" read *Adeenanugur*.

63—last line but one, for "*Pathun Kot*" read *Puthan Kot*.

76—eleventh line, for "*Feelor*" read *Philor*.

82—tenth line, for "*Huttoo*" read *Athoo*.

82—twelfth line, for "*Dushut*" read *Duskut*.

94—ninth line from the bottom, for "*Jihlum*" read *Jyhlum*.

145—fourth line from the top, for "*Qootub ood deen*" read *Kootub ood deen*.

162—eleventh line, for "*Gorchur*" read *Ghorchur*.

185—fourth and fifth lines from the bottom, for "*Gorchur*" read *Ghorchur*.

CONTENTS.

CHAPTER I.

CHAPTER II.

CHAPTER III.

CHAPTER IV.

CHAPTER X.

CHAPTER XI.

APPENDIX.

CHAPTER FIRST.*

A. D. 1742 to 1761.

Affairs of the Punjab on the decline of the Dehlee Sovereignty to the Battle of Paneeput and separation of the territory from Hindoostan.

THE empire founded in Hindoostan by BABUR, and supported by the vigour and abilities of several generations of celebrated Princes, fell speedily to dissolution after the accession of MOHUMMUD SHAH. The invasion of NADIR SHAH gave a violent shock to its stability, which was already undermined by the growing power of the Mahrattas; and the inroads of the Abdalee, AHMED SHAH, though made in support of the faith of MOHUMMUD, and successful in checking that reaction of Hindoo vigour, which threatened at the time to overwhelm it, accelerated nevertheless the fall of the house of TYMOOR,

* This Chapter is entirely from Captain MURRAY, who has the merit of being the first to collect and put together in a consistent narrative, the loose fragments and materials that exist, in respect to the events in the Punjab at this period.

which he uniformly treated with neglect and humiliation. The court of Dehlee ceased thenceforward to be looked up to as the source of protection, of honors, or of punishments. The satraps, and officers, nominally acting under its authority, assumed every where independence: the provinces were dismembered, and a spirit of disaffection was roused in all parts of the empire. The history of Hindoostan ceases from this period to be that of any ruling dynasty, and must be traced in the detail of the events of each province, and in the transactions, by which the several Nuwabs, Rajas, and Princes,—the sects, nations or associations of chiefs, rose each in turn to power, in displacement of the royal authority, and in successful rivalry with one another. It is the object of the following pages to collect and exhibit in continuous narrative, the occurrences of this description in the Punjab, and to trace the rise of the chief who now sways the destinies of that province, and of a large bordering territory, with a vigour of authority, unknown to any other part of India, not subject to the dominion of Europeans.

YUHEEA KHAN, the son of ZUKAREEA KHAN, commonly styled KHAN BUHADOOR, held the viceroyalty of Lahôr, when the Jât Zumeendars of the Punjab empoverished by long extortion, and driven at last to desperation, took to rapine and plunder for the support of themselves and families, and as a bond of union and excitement against their oppressors revived in their customs and ceremonies, the latent flame of the Sikh ritual. They proclaimed the faith and tenets of GOVIND SINGH, the last acknowledged *Gooroo* or spiritual guide of the Sikhs, and took the *Pahul* of initiation into the mysteries of that religion. The long hair on the head, and flowing beard, the entire renunciation of tobacco, and the use of the audible salutation of "*Wah Gooroo-jee ke futeh,*" (victory to Gooroo jee,) proclaimed that the ploughshare had been exchanged for the avenger's sword, and that the maxims and precepts of the *grunth* of GOOROO GOVIND had prevailed over the more peaceable doctrines of the *vedas* and *shastras* of pure Hindooism. The spirit of the revived sect displayed itself at first in secret association and isolated acts of depredation. Bodies of armed men, in tens and twenties, called *Dharwee* in the dialect of the province, that is, highwaymen, infested the routes of communication, attacked villages or plundered in towns, according as their local connections invited to either mode of seeking wealth or the means of support. The early neglect of the ruling authority enabled the associations to prosper, and the most successful chiefs purchased horses with the proceeds of their spoil, and mounted and armed their followers. Their example and success made the cause popular with the young and adventurous, so that the number who took to these courses augmented daily, until the chiefs formed their respective *dehras* or encampments in open defiance of the ruling authority, and sought celebrity by bold and hardy enterprizes, which gave security in the awe they inspired, while the wealth and reputation resulting afforded the means of further strengthening themselves. The distractions of the Moghul empire, and the intrigues and imbecilities of the vice-regal court at Lahôr, gave encouragement to the system pursued, not only by the neglect to punish, but by the occasional availment of the services of individual chiefs, so that many of them assumed an organized martial appearance, and not content with ravaging the open country, approached the sacred reservoir of the Sikhs at Umritsur and maintained themselves in that vicinity. The different associations were united by common interest, no less than by the profession of a new faith; and a system of general confederation for defence, or for operations requiring more than single efforts, was early arranged between the chiefs.

The evil had spread and had acquired some head before the attention of the Governor YUHEEA KHAN was sufficiently roused to induce him to make an exertion to put it down. At length, however, his revenue failing from these disorders, he sent out a small detachment of government troops under command of JUSPUT RAEE, brother of his Dewan or prime minister, LUKHPUT RAEE. They proceeded first against a body of insurgent Sikhs who were devastating the country, and driving off the flocks and herds in the vicinity of Yumeenabad, which lies to the North of Lahôr. The detachment was overpowered, and JUSPUT RAEE being slain, his men dispersed. LUKHPUT RAEE Dewan, however, hastened from Lahôr to avenge his brother's death, and the insurgents retreated before him into the north eastern corner of the Punjab, where he inflicted on them a severe chastisement. The Dewan brought back with him many prisoners, whose heads were struck off without remorse in the *Ghora-Nukhas,* or horse market, outside the city wall of Lahôr. The spot is now called by the Sikhs "*Shuheed-gunj,*" the place of martyrs, in memory of this event, and a *sumadh* or tomb has been erected there in honor of the Bhaee JAROO SINGH, which marks the site. After this success a proclamation was issued in the name of the Governor YUHEEA KHAN, denouncing death to all persons who invoked the name of GOOROO GOVIND, and a reward was offered for the heads of his disciples. This rigour and summary proscription checked the progress of Sikh proselytism, and the enthusiasm of the votaries of the Gooroo was considerably diminished. Many cut their long hair and curtailed their flowing beards to avoid detection and death, and others fled across the Sutlej into the adjoining province of Sirhind, where they found protection or concealment in the wide wastes which lie to the west of Putccala and Naba.

Not long after this event, the younger brother of YUHEEA KHAN, by name SHAH NUWAZ KHAN, rose in insurrection against him, and succeeded in establishing himself in the two provinces of Lahôr and Mooltan, making prisoner YUHEEA KHAN, with all his state officers. He nominated a Hindoo, named KAONRA MUL, to be Dewan in lieu of LUKHPUT RAEE, but left ADEENA BEG KHAN, who had risen under his father ZUKAREEA KHAN, and governed with much vigour the difficult district of the Jalundhur Dooab, in both civil and military charge of that tract. YUHEEA KHAN escaped from Lahôr, and hastening to Dehlee, laid his complaint before the Vuzeer, his uncle KUMUR-OOD-DEEN KHAN, who was at the same time privately informed, that SHAH NUWAZ KHAN, in fear of the consequences of his act, had opened a correspondence with AHMED SHAH Abdalee. The Shah had recently seized Kabool and Peshawur in ejection of the Dehlee Soobahdar, NASIR KHAN, an event that had excited much alarm at the capital. The Vuzeer availing himself of his relationship appealed to his nephew's sense of honor, and addressed to him a strong remonstrance on his defection from allegiance, desiring him not to seek the degradation of serving Ahmed, the *gussool* or mace-bearer of Nadir, but to be faithful to the hereditary sovereign of his family and race. The young man's pride was touched, and although doubtful what might be the issue of the complaint of his elder brother, he prepared himself to oppose the advance of the Dooranees, and withdrew from further correspondence with Ahmed Shah. Undeterred by this change of counsels, the Abdalee crossed the Indus near the fort of Attuk, in the year 1747, and sent his domestic priest, Sabir Shah, in advance to Lahôr, hoping through his negotiations or intrigues to bind Shah Nuwaz Khan to his first offers, or at all events to secure a friendly reception to his army. Shah Nuwaz, however, was now staunch in his allegiance to Dehlee, and placed himself in the best posture of defence his scanty means would permit. He further gave to his court a pledge of fidelity by causing the agent of the Abdalee to be murdered. Ahmed Shah was greatly incensed at this violence done to the person of his ambassador and confidential servant, and crossing the Ravee, marched immediately to attack Shah Nuwaz Khan in the entrenched position he had taken up under the walls of Lahôr. The resistance offered was slight; the defences were soon mastered by the Dooranee warriors, and Shah Nuwaz escaping fled to Dehlee; the city of Lahôr was shortly after reduced, and its resources fell a prey to the Abdalee, who raised there a heavy contribution.

Ahmed Shah when at Dehlee in the train of Nadir Shah, had not been an inattentive observer of the state of things at that Court. The imbecility of Mohummud

SHAH, the overgrown power, the discords and intrigues of the great Ameers or grandees, and the little obedience paid to the royal authority at the capital as well as in the interior, had not failed to attract his attention, and the confusion likely to follow the departure of the invading army, afforded matter of speculation for an ambitious man seeking where eventually to push his own fortune. The unparalleled success which had attended his first efforts in Afghanistan, and the advantage to which he systematically turned his present means in laying the foundation of future grandeur, encouraged him to hope from what he saw and heard of the condition of things at Dehlee, that the time was favorable for an attempt to erect for himself an empire on the ruins of that of the house of TYMOOR. Having mastered Lahôr, therefore, he determined on an immediate advance towards Dehlee, and crossing the Beah and Sutlej without opposition, approached Sirhind.

The Vuzeer KUMUR-OOD-DEEN KHAN was not deficient in energy, and made preparation to meet the invader. Calling out the principal chiefs of Rajpootana with their respective quotas, he placed the king's eldest son Prince AHMED in nominal command, and with this force and the troops at the capital took up an intrenched position at the village of Munoopoor, nine miles from Sirhind. The Abdalee Shah having reconnoitered the position deemed himself too weak to attempt a storm of the works: encamping in the neighbourhood therefore, he directed his efforts against the supplies of the Dehlee army, and sent detachments to cut off convoys and intercept the communications with the capital. This led to continual skirmishes and partial engagements, which amused both armies for a month without producing any thing decisive. An event however then occurred that brought about an immediate change in the aspect of things. The Vuzeer was killed whilst at evening prayers by a random shot from the Dooranee artillery, and from that time forward there ceased to be any commander in chief in the Dehlee camp. The Rajpoot chiefs who had come upon his invitation, and were held together by his influence and reputation, feeling confidence in no other leader, began to desert the royal standard, and retired to their respective estates. The Abdalee hearing of this deemed the moment favorable to assume the offensive, and ordered an attack, notwithstanding the inferiority of his numbers. A panic fell on the imperial army and disorder began to spread in the camp. MEER MUNOO, however, son of the deceased Vuzeer, seized the critical moment, and bringing a body of fresh troops to the points assailed, led them himself to the charge, and repulsed the Dooranees with considerable slaughter; so much so that AHMED SHAH deemed it necessary to relinquish his designs for the present, and retired precipitately across the Punjab in order to repair his losses. His retreat was unmolested, and he recrossed the Attuk without making any effort to maintain his footing at Lahôr. The Punjab was thus recovered for the Moghul, and the Government of Lahôr and Mooltan was conferred by the Dehlee Court on MEER MUNOO, with the title of MOOYYUNOOL-MOOLK, in reward and acknowledgment of his service on this important occasion.

The invasion of the Abdalee, and the occupation of the forces on both sides in the struggle for empire on the plains of Sirhind, were favorable to the further rise of the Sikhs, whose depredations were for the interval unchecked, and who again showed themselves by day, and ventured even to satisfy their religious prejudices by stolen visits to the shrines of their faith at Umritsur. The new Governor of Lahôr, MEER MUNOO, confirmed KAONRA MUL in the office of Dewan, and found the disorders created by these associations, and by fanatics of the sect who sprung up in numbers, to be one of the first objects requiring his attention. A small party of Sikhs had the audacity to throw up a mud work which they called Ram-Rounee, (but which having been since enlarged is now called Ramgurh) in the district and immediate vicinity of Umritsur, and Sikh plunderers scoured the country in all directions. MEER MUNOO surrounded and captured Ram-Rounee, and stationed detachments to preserve the peace of the country, who had orders to detain all Sikhs, and to shave their heads and beards. By these energetic measures the public confidence was restored: the Sikhs were again compelled to fly the country or hide their heads, and proselytes to their faith and habits became more rare.

AHMED SHAH Abdalee had retired only to recruit his strength, and was by no means inclined to relinquish his designs on Hindoostan. In the following season from that of his first invasion, that is, after the close of the rains of 1748, he again crossed the Indus, and interrupted all MEER MUNOO's plans for establishing himself in his government and better ordering its administration. Being apprehensive that his force was too weak to resist the invader, he applied to Dehlee for reinforcements, and in order to gain time sent a mission to the Abdalee camp to offer terms of compromise and negociate for the Shah's retirement. He followed up this measure by himself moving out of Lahôr, and pitched his camp at Soudhura, on the south bank of the Chunâb. This state of preparation and the known character of the Lahôr viceroy deterred the Abdalee for the time from attempting to force his way into Hindostan. He was content therefore to accept a promise of the revenue of the four districts, Pursuroor, Goojrat, Seâl-Kot, and Aurungabad, which had formerly been assigned to NADIR SHAH, and then retraced his steps to Kabool.

This success of MEER MUNOO and the credit resulting excited envy in the grandees at Dehlee, and instead of meeting further reward from the court, an intrigue there deprived him of the government of Mooltan, which was conferred on SHAH NUWAZ KHAN. The viceroy in possession, however, was not of a temper to submit patiently to such supercession, and he detached his minister KAONRA MUL to oppose the new governor. SHAH NUWAZ KHAN advanced to the frontier of Mooltan, with a force collected for the purpose of securing his investiture, but finding himself overmatched could proceed no farther. For about six months he maintained himself on the frontier without any thing decisive occurring, but at the end of that time he was induced to hazard a battle with the Dewan, in which he was defeated and slain. MEER MUNOO created KAONRA MUL Raja for this service, and invested him with the subordinate charge of Mooltan and the adjoining districts.

As might be expected, MEER MUNOO failed to remit to Kabool the revenues of the four districts stipulated, and the Abdalee AHMED SHAH had thus a pretext for again crossing the Indus, which he did in the season 1751-2, and advanced to the right bank of the Chunab. SOOKH JEEWUN, a Hindoo, was sent thence to Lahôr to demand the fulfilment of the engagement. MEER MUNOO replied, that the promise had been made in the exigency of the moment, and he did not look upon himself as bound to abide by the strict letter, but free to act according to circumstances. He offered, however, to pay now what might be due, upon the condition of the Dooranee army being immediately withdrawn. Not expecting this offer to be accepted, MEER MUNOO called in ADEENA BEG KHAN and Raja KAONRA MUL with their respective forces, to Lahôr, where an intrenched camp was prepared at Shahdurra in the environs. He himself advanced to meet the Abdalee, and retired before him as he moved eastward until both chiefs approached Lahôr, when the viceroy entered his entrenched position under the walls of the city. For four months he maintained himself in this post, and was proof against every endeavour of the Shah to entice him out of his entrenchment. The blockade maintained was however strict, and supplies then began wholly to fail. The only food or forage for the horses and ammunition cattle consisted of chopped straw from the roofs of huts and bazars, and grain and flour were selling at an exorbitant price. A council of war was called in this emergency, when ADEENA BEG gave it as his opinion that as no succour or reinforcement could be expected from Dehlee, an action ought to be risked before their provisions wholly failed, as might be expected in a few days, if the blockade continued. Raja KAONRA MUL was opposed to this advice, he observed that the Viceroy's troops were mostly raw levies, who were no match in the field for the hardy veterans of the Shah. That the country for a wide space round had been foraged and wasted, and the distress for provisions was not less in the Dooranee camp than in their own—that in twenty days more the hot weather would set in, when the northern troops of the Shah would find the sun and wind intolerable in the plains, and hence would be compelled to retreat or to attack them in their lines to disadvantage. There can be no doubt that the advice of the Hindoo was the preferable and more prudent course, but the viceroy was young, and not free from the impatience and impetuosity of youth, and the opinion of ADEENA BEG fell more in accordance with his own disposition. Early in the morning therefore of the 12th April 1752, his army moved from its lines and took up ground on an elevated spot marked by an old brick-kiln. The Shah prepared immediately for action. His artillery was ordered to advance, and a cannonade was kept up between the two armies until the afternoon, when the Shah observing some confusion ordered a charge by a select body of cavalry, which was so far successful as to induce MEER MUNOO to retire again within his entrenchments. In the retreat Raja KAONRA MUL'S elephant chanced to tread on an old grave, the earth of which sinking strained and nearly disabled the animal. Before the Mahout could extricate him, the Raja was overtaken and slain by a Dooranee horseman, and his loss, when it came to be known in the entrenched camp, occasioned a panic and desertion so general, that the viceroy was compelled, by diminished numbers, to retire within the city wall. In this exigency ADEENA BEG KHAN abruptly withdrew with his troops, and MEER MUNOO, finding the fortifications of the city out of repair and untenable, was induced to yield to circumstances, and tendered his submission to the Shah.

The Abdalee was well pleased so to close the campaign: he sent his principal officer, JUHAN KHAN, into the city, to conduct the viceroy to his presence, and treated him with all courtesy and respect, declaring his admiration of the determined spirit, conduct and deportment displayed by him on all occasions. He exacted a large sum of money from him for the expences of the campaign, and then reinstated him as viceroy on his own part both of Lahôr and Mooltan.

Before retiring to his own dominions, AHMED SHAH determined on the occupation of Kashmeer, and a strong detachment was sent thither under command of UBDOOLLA KHAN, who succeeded in penetrating to the valley, and establishing the Shah's authority there without opposition. The Hindoo, SOOKH-JEEWUN, a Khutree of Kabool, was selected for the government, and the rainy season being now near, the Shah re-crossed the Indus, and carried back his army to Kabool.

MEER MUNOO did not long survive these events: he was killed by a fall from his horse, whereupon his widow, a woman of spirit and address, proclaimed her infant son as successor in the viceroyalty, and succeeded in establishing an administration in his name. Before ten months had expired, however, this hope was likewise cut off, the infant dying of the small pox. The Begum then proclaimed her own name, and dispatched agents to Dehlee and to Kabool to procure her acknowledgment. To the Vuzeer at Dehlee her daughter was offered in marriage, and he came to the banks of the Sutlej to celebrate the nuptials. By these acts the Begum secured herself against present supercession, and her authority was displayed in an act of cruelty, the motives of which have left a taint of scandal on her reputation. Upon the accusation of having designs upon the viceroyalty, MEER BHEKAREE KHAN, an influential officer of the late viceroy, was seized by her order, and carried into the interior apartments, where he was so severely beaten with shoes and sticks as to expire under the punishment. The Begum's personal concern in such an act gave credit to the imputation, very generally believed at the time, that it was committed in revenge for some personal disappointment of a kind never forgiven by a woman.

A female viceroy was not likely to display much activity in suppressing associations like those of the Sikhs, which meddled not with her ease and pleasures at the seat of government. Their number and audacity accordingly increased rapidly, and bands of these bearded depredators were continually to be seen, traversing the various districts of the Punjab, sweeping off the flocks and herds, and laying waste the cultivation, unless redeemed by a prompt contribution. Disorder, anarchy, and confusion gained head in the province, as in all other parts of Hindoostan.

It was not until after an interval of four years, that is, in the season 1755-6, that AHMED SHAH Abdalee appeared again in the field. In all his previous incursions he had been met by the energy of local governors, and the Dehlee court had made efforts, or at least had displayed some interest and anxiety in checking his advance. On the present occasion, such was the condition of wreck and revolution to which the empire was reduced, that no one offered any where to impede his march, and he traversed the Punjab and entered even the imperial city without experiencing the smallest opposition. His detachments plundered Muthra and threatened the city of Agra, and the Shah having formed a matrimonial connexion with the family of TYMOOR, laid the capital under heavy contribution, and confiscated to his own use the property of the grandees and principal inhabitants. His cupidity being thus satisfied, he retired, leaving the throne of the Moghul in the same weak hands, and helpless condition in which he found it. But he seized on the Punjab and Sirhind, and gave the government of both provinces to his son TYMOOR, with whom he left his confidential officer JUHAN KHAN and a detachment of troops of no great strength, and then returned to Kabool.

Since the death of MEER MUNOO, ADEENA BEG KHAN had assumed entire independence in his subordinate government in the Jalundhur Dooab, and had appropriated the revenues to his personal use and in providing the means of maintaining himself. One of the first acts of the young Prince TYMOOR was to summon this chief to Lahôr as a dependant of his government. The wary veteran however evaded prompt compliance, alleging the necessity of his presence in his districts to check the increasing audacity of the Sikhs who were encamped in his vicinity, and, were he to desert his post, might secure a permanent hold in the country. The Afghan Prince not satisfied with this excuse, sent a detachment of his troops to seize ADEENA BEG, whereupon the latter strengthened himself by association with the Sikhs, of whom he took a considerable body into pay, and with them retired before the Afghans into the northern hills. Being now fully committed with the Dooranees, his mind, fertile in resources, sought the means of succour and relief in a quarter, which would not readily have occurred to another. He applied to the Muhrattas, whose reputation for enterprize and daring adventure was then high, and whose chiefs were at the time encamped near Dehlee. He stipulated for the payment of a daily sum for their aid, and pointed out the rich harvest of spoil that was within their reach. The expedition was entered upon with alacrity, and MULHAR RAO HOLKUR, with some other chiefs of that nation, marched immediately for the Punjab, where they were joined on passing the Sutlej by ADEENA BEG, with a swarm of Sikh plunderers, and the whole advanced rapidly on Lahôr. The Prince TYMOOR and JUHAN KHAN were unable to stem this torrent of invasion, and retired precipitately to the Indus. Their retreat was harassed by frequent attacks, and most of their baggage taken. The Muhrattas then overran the whole country, and their main body returned to Dehlee, but a detachment of this nation was left in the occupation of Lahôr.

ADEENA BEG KHAN did not long survive this event. He died in 1758, having latterly, and indeed for a long time, played a very conspicuous part in the diplomacy of the Punjab and Hindoostan. His address, experience, and extensive knowledge recommended him early to the notice of the viceroys, who in succession ruled Lahôr: under them he rose through the gradations of office, until his services were at last recompensed by the delegated administration of a troublesome but very fertile region. During a season of unusual disorder and difficulty, he maintained his station, and kept his territory prosperous and profitable: while in the midst of struggles for dominion between contending nations, and in the conflict of parties, and the intrigues of chiefs, all stronger than himself, he contrived to acquire something at every change, and availed himself of every opportunity to aggrandize and strengthen his power, with a depth of cunning, and a readiness which gained for him a high reputation for wisdom. He was a master of the arts and shifts of Indian diplomacy. The Sikhs he amused, and secured immunity from their depredations, by occasionally paying for their services, and he would even buy their forbearance when too weak to coerce them. When his ruin was determined upon by the Abdalee Afghans, he bribed the Muhrattas to enter the field against them, and by this means effected the expulsion of the prince, who drove him to such extremity, together with his minister, whom he suspected as the instigator of the mischief. How he would have played his part in the great struggle impending between the Muhrattas and Abdalee Afghans can only be surmised, death having saved him from the vengeance or politic mercy of the Shah. He left no issue or successor to perpetuate his name and authority, but his memory lives in the Punjab, and he is respected even by the Sikhs as the last of the Moghul rulers in their country.

The Muhrattas were now the ruling power of Hindoostan; their forces traversed the country, from the Dukhun to the Indus, and Himalaya, and no one ventured to take the field against them. The Moosulman Soobahdars, who had asserted independence, in the decadence of the Moghul empire, trembled for their principalities, and seemed to have no alternative but submission, and the payment of Chout to this upstart

Hindoo sovereignty, or absolute extinction. In this state of things the re-appearance of the Abdalee, AHMED SHAH, east of the Indus, was hailed by a large party in Hindoostan as a source of salvation, and welcome succour. SHOOJA-OOD-DOULA, in Oudh, the celebrated NUJEEB-OOD-DOULA, who governed Dehlee and the Northern Dooab, the Rohilla Chiefs, and all the Mohummedan families settled in the Dooab, or west of the Jumna, prepared to range themselves under the standard of the Shah, and to fight the great battle for their faith and independence under his leading. The Muhratta detachment retired before the Shah from Lahôr to Dehlee, pillaging and laying waste the country as they went. The fertile plains of Sirhind consequently exhibited an appearance of desolation, that induced the Abdalee, as well for the convenience of obtaining supplies, as to unite with the Mohummedan chiefs of Hindoostan, to cross the Jumna at Boorea into the Dooab. Here he fell in with and overpowered a Mahratta detachment under DUTTAJEE SINDHEEA who was slain, and MULHAR RAO HOLKUR was overtaken soon after by two Afghan generals, who routed his troops, and had nearly taken the chief himself by surprise. When the rainy season approached, the Abdalee cantoned his army in the Dooab between Sekundra and Anoopshuhur, the country round Dehlee, and to the west of the Jumna, having been completely ravaged and laid waste by the Muhrattas.

The court of Poona on being apprised of the arrival of the Shah, and of the defeat of DUTTAJEE SINDHEEA and MULHAR RAO HOLKUR, prepared for a great effort to maintain their supremacy in Hindoostan. The retainers of the state were called out, and an immense army advanced towards Dehlee, under the command of SUDASHEEO RAO BHAO, commonly called the Bhâo, with whom went WISWAS RAO, the PESHWA's eldest son, and the heads of all the principal Muhratta families. On the march the chiefs in advance fell in and swelled the train, and the whole reached Dehlee, pillaging without remorse as they went, and encountering no where any opposition.

The Jumna which divided the two armies was still unfordable, and the Bhâo, after a short halt at Dehlee' moved northward to Kurnal, where his army was occupied for a few days in the siege of Koonjpoora, the possession of a Puthan family, on the west bank of the Jumna. The place was taken by storm after an obstinate resistance by the head of the family, NIJABUT KHAN, who was slain in the last assault. The Mahratta army then moved back on Paneeput, and allowed the Shah to ford the Jumna with all his cavalry, on the 23d of October. The Bhâo judged himself to be unequal to cope with the Shah in the open field; he accordingly threw up intrenchments and took up a position about the town of Paneeput, and there waited the attack of the enemy. The Abdalee strengthened by the junction of the confederate forces of Oudh, Rohilkhund, and of all the Mohummedan Chiefs of upper Hindoostan, surrounded the Mahrattas, and aimed to cut off the Bhâo's supplies. For three months, the two armies lay close to each other, occupied in skirmishes and partial actions, and the Shah maintained his blockade. At the end of this time, want began to be felt in the Bhâo's lines, and the distress from this cause increased to such a degree as to compel the Bhâo to risk an action. On the 7th of January 1761, he led his army out of their intrenched position at day break, and prepared for the final struggle. The Muhrattas were entirely defeated, and both WISWAS RAO and the Bhâo were slain in the action, with many other principal Muhratta chiefs. There have been few battles attended with greater carnage than history assigns to this. The lowest computation of the loss sustained by the Muhrattas, fixes the number engaged at 200,000, of whom more than half were slain in the action or pursuit: and, considering how far from their own country they fought, and that the intermediate tract was mostly hostile, our wonder at the loss will be lessened. But the moral effect on the Muhratta nation was greater even than the actual loss. Their entire force had been put forth for the struggle, and defeat was for the moment felt as the annihilation of their ambitious hopes, and the destruction of their power.

The Abdalee remained for a few days after this important victory in the city of Dehlee regulating the affairs of Hindoostan. He then returned through the Punjab to Kabool, appointing KHAJA OBYD and ZYN KHAN to be his governors in Lahôr and Sirhind, which he designed permanently to annex to his own dominions.

CHAPTER SECOND.*

A. D. 1761 to 1771.

Operations of the Afghans in the Punjab. The condition of the Sikh associations, and the rise and exploits of the principal Chiefs and Misuls. The Punjab abandoned to them by the Afghans. Their proceedings for the occupation of the territory.

AHMED SHAH made no stay in the Punjab, and troubled himself little with the disorders that prevailed in its internal administration. The governor he left at Lahôr was little better than the military commandant of an out-post, collecting revenues and levying contributions as he could, for the support of his detachment, and in aid of the general resources of the Shah. The imperfect hold thus retained of this territory, and the weakness of the detachment left with the Afghan governor, KHAJA OBYD, were highly favorable to the Sikhs, who throve upon the disorder which prevailed; and, in the neglect with which they were treated, secured strong holds and fastnesses in different parts of the country, and added greatly to their

* In this Chapter several facts have been added to Captain MURRAY'S Narrative, on the authority of the Report of Captain WADE, whose information as to the origin of the family of RUNJEET SINGH, will have been derived from the most authentic sources.

power and resources. Amongst others, the ancestors of RUNJEET SINGH, the present ruler of the Punjab, appeared early in the field as leaders of enterprize, and acquired a reputation that was daily on the increase. The family boasts of no antiquity, the first of whom any traditionary recollection is preserved was a petty Zumeendar, named DESOO, a Jath, of the Sânsee tribe, who resided in a village of the district of Manjha, called Sookur-chuk. His patrimony was confined to three ploughs and a well, and little is known of him, except that he was the father of NODH SINGH, whose son CHURUT SINGH, founded the fortunes of the family, by establishing a Surdaree or chieftainship, which his descendants, MUHA SINGH and RUNJEET, have improved into the sovereignty over a wide and fertile territory.

NODH SINGH was the first of the family who embraced the Sikh religion: he sought in marriage the daughter of GOOLAB SINGH, a Zumeendar of Mejithia, who was already initiated in the rites of that faith, and the Pahul was proposed as the condition of the nuptials. NODH SINGH yielded; and, after his marriage, gave up his father's plough, and purchasing, or otherwise procuring a horse, joined the association headed by KAPOOR SINGH, of Goojrat, which bore the title of Fyzoollapoorea.

NODH SINGH is stated to have died in 1750; when CHURUT SINGH, following his father's courses, but disdaining to serve in a subordinate capacity, associated with himself his brothers-in-law DUL SINGH and JODH SINGH, and with their help, raised some followers, whom he maintained and kept together by successful predatory enterprizes. His wife was of Gujuraolee, a village lying not far north of Lahôr, and through the influence of her family, he obtained leave to erect in its vicinity a small mud fort to serve as a place of safe custody for his plunder, and of retreat for his family and followers. The post was convenient, from its vicinity to Lahôr, as a rallying point for other Sikh associations; and in 1762, it attracted the attention of KHAJA OBYD, who marched with a force to raise it and eject CHURUT SINGH from the neighbourhood. The Sikhs, however, attached importance to the post, and a large body tendered their aid for its defence. When the governor approached Gujuraolee, they threw a select body into the gurhee, and hovering about, watched his camp. KHAJA OBYD had entertained for the enterprize a number of Sikh troops, who opened a clandestine correspondence with their brethren, and ultimately deserted in a body to the enemy. The governor's other troops immediately took panic and dispersed, and KHAJA OBYD himself had barely time to mount a fleet horse and escape, when the Sikhs broke into his camp and plundered all his baggage.

After this defeat, the Afghan governor dared scarcely to show himself beyond the walls of Lahôr; and the Sikh Dul, or assembly of chiefs and followers, was publicly held at Umritsur, where the bathings and other ceremonies of the Dewalee being performed, it was resolved to invest Jundeeala, a place held by NERUNJUNEE GOOROO, a Hindoo, who had made submission and taken service with AHMED SHAH, and hence had incurred the vengeance of the votaries of GOOROO GOVIND.

The report of these events roused the attention of AHMED SHAH, who, in November 1762, again appeared on the Indus. From thence he made, with a select detachment, one of those long and rapid marches, for which he was celebrated, in the hope of surprising the Sikhs, who had invested, and were still employed in the siege of Jundeeala. They obtained, however, a few hour's notice of his approach, and breaking up their camp, dispersed in different directions, most of them flying beyond the Sutlej. The Shah rejoined his main body at Lahôr, and ordered his governor of Sirhind to watch the Sikhs, and call out the several Moosulman Sirdars and Jageerdars, with their contingents, to operate against them. The Shah was informed by express soon after this, that the main body of the Sikhs was at Kos Ruheera, on the south bank of the Sutlej, (whose course from Feerozpoor is from east to west,) and that ZYN KHAN, with the Baraich and Mulêr Kotila Moosulmans, was watching their movements. The Shah immediately prepared a strong detachment of cavalry provisioned for three days; and, leaving Lahôr as secretly as possible, led them himself against the enemy. On the evening of the second day he crossed the Sutlej, and made a halt of a few hours only at Loodeeana. By sunrise on the following morning he joined ZYN KHAN, and found him already engaged with the Sikhs, for these latter trusting to their great numerical superiority had thought to overpower the Sirhind governor, and attacked him in his camp. The appearance of the high sheep-skin caps of the Shah's body-guard and northern troops, gave an immediate turn to the battle, and the Sikhs were broken and fled. The pursuit was continued west as far as Hureeana-Burnulla, and the slaughter was great. It has been estimated at from 25 to 30,000 men, but Captain MURRAY states he was assured by an old Moosulman of

Mulêr Kotila, who was in the action, that the entire killed and wounded of the Sikhs in this battle did not exceed 12,000. The want of muster-rolls and the irregular formation of Indian armies, which are always mere associations of chiefs, all representing their force larger than the reality, must necessarily make it difficult, if not impossible, ever to ascertain the real loss sustained in action. This disaster is however characterised in Sikh tradition, as the *Ghuloo-Ghara* or bloody carnage. ALA SINGH, of Puteeala, chief of the Phool family, was made prisoner at Burnala, and carried by the Shah to Lahôr. There, at the intercession of SHAH WULEE KHAN the minister, he was released upon an engagement to pay tribute, and his manly conduct and demeanour having secured him the Shah's favor, he was honored with the title of Raja, and dismissed with a rich dress of state.

The Shah in irritation against the sect for the trouble they had given him, not less than from bigotted zeal against all idolators and infidels, signalized his march through Umritsur, by the demolition of the Sikh temple of Hurmundur and of the sacred reservoir. The first was blown up with gun-powder, and the reservoir, besides being defaced and filled up as far as materials and time permitted, was polluted with the blood and entrails of cows and bullocks, a sacrilege even greater in the eyes of the schismatic disciple of GOOROO GOVIND than of the orthodox Brahminical Hindoo.

The Shah's attention was now turned towards Kashmeer, where his Governor SOOKH JEEWUN had for nine years conducted the administration without remitting any portion of the revenues to the Royal treasury.

The co-operation of RUNJEET DEO, Raja of Jummoo, having been secured with some difficulty, a strong detachment was sent from Lahôr under command of NOOR-OOD-DEEN, and the Raja conducted it across the Peer Punjal mountains into the valley, which submitted after a slight resistance. SOOKH JEEWUN being made prisoner, was punished with the loss of his eyes. AHMED SHAH having made these arrangements to secure his territory east of the Indus, returned to Ḳabool at the end of the year 1762. He left KABULEE MUL, a Hindoo, as his Governor of Lahôr.

No sooner had the Abdalee departed, than the Sikhs re-appeared in the field. A Goormutta, or council of the sect, was held publicly at Umritsur, and a large body of them marched thence to Kusoor, (or Kâsoor,) which was taken and sacked, and yielded a considerable booty. Elate with this success they collected a larger force, and determined on the attack of Sirhind. They appeared before the place with 40,000 men, who encamped in two divisions, to the east and west of the town. In the month of December 1763, the Governor ZYN KHAN moved out to risk an action with the Sikhs. The forces joined battle at Peer Zyn Munayra, a village about seven miles east of Sirhind, when fortune favored the Sikhs, and the Moosulman leaders were slain. The town of Sirhind was then carried, and most of the buildings razed to the ground, the Sikh animosity against the place being excited by the recollection, that the wife and infant son of their saint GOOROO GOVIND had there been inhumanly put to death by VUZEER KHAN, the governor for Aurungzeeb. Not a house was left standing, and it is even to this day deemed a meritorious act by a

Sikh, to pull down three bricks from any standing wall of Sirhind, and convey them to the Sutlej or Jumna to be cast there into the river.

The audacity of this enterprize recalled AHMED SHAH to Lahôr, he re-appeared there in January 1764, being his seventh invasion of Hindoostan. His arrival was the signal for the Sikhs to disperse and seek refuge in the deserts west and south of Puteeala and Nabah. Raja ALA SINGH, of the former place, had obtained the ruins of Sirhind from the Joomla chief, BHAEE BOODHA SINGH, to whom the town had been assigned by unanimous vote of the chiefs who made the capture, the Raja giving him a few productive villages in exchange. By the influence of the minister, SHAH WULEE KHAN, he obtained from the Shah a confirmation of his tenure. The disorders which prevailed were matter of deep regret to the Abdalee, but the means or time was wanting for their effectual cure, and he retraced his steps to Kabool, without having done anything for the punishment or suppression of the Sikhs. He was no sooner gone, than they collected again, and ventured to attack Lahôr. KABULEE MUL was compelled to fly, and the city being mastered, was parcelled out by the captors in three divisions, which were assigned respectively to LEHNA SINGH, GOOJUR SINGH, and SOBHA. AHMED SHAH returned to punish this outrage, and advanced as far as the Sutlej, the Sikhs flying before him to the deserts south of the Ingraon, and no enemy appearing on whom he could wreak his vengeance. On his arrival at the Sutlej, UMUR SINGH, the grandson of Raja ALA SINGH, then recently deceased, waited upon him, and received investiture with the title of Muha-Raja-Rajugan-Muhindur

Buhadur, which title is now borne by the head of the Puteeala family. In the midst of these operations a Dusta, or body of 12,000 of the Shah's army, suddenly quitted his camp without orders. and marched back to Kabool. The Shah followed to reclaim or punish them, but his retreat was harrassed by parties of Sikhs, who plundered much of his baggage, and hung on his flanks and rear until he had passed the Chunab.

The Shah having thus quitted the field, the Sikhs remained undisputed masters of the Punjab, and spreading over the country occupied it as a permanent inheritance, every Sirdar, according to his strength, seizing what fell in his way, and acknowledging no superior, nor submitting to the control of any body, nor to any constituted authority whatsoever. Their proceedings were unmolested by any further interference from the west, where AHMED SHAH continued to reign until his death in 1773, from a cancer in his face. His son and successor TYMOOR enjoyed his throne in peace for twenty years, and made no attempt to recover Lahôr, and the Punjab. These, with the province of Sirhind, and the country east as far as the Jumna, fell into the possession of the chiefs and associations who had hitherto subsisted on plunder, and were for the most part of low origin, and wholly deficient in education and useful knowledge.

The Sirdars or chiefs of the Sikh nation had been followed into the field by relations, friends, and volunteers, and not ordinarily by hired retainers. Most of these looked upon themselves as partners and associates in each enterprize, and regarded the lands now acquired as a common property in which each was to have his share, according to the degree in which he might have contributed to the acquisition. The associations were called *Misuls*, implying that they were confederacies of equals, under chiefs of their own selection. The chief was to lead in war, and act as arbiter in peace: he was respected and treated with deference by the inferior Sirdars, but these owned no obligation to obey, beyond what they might consider to be for their own reciprocal benefit, or for the well being of the Misul. The confederacies had each their distinguishing title, and at this period there are twelve principal Misuls enumerated, which together could bring into the field about 70,000 horse. The following is a recapitulation of them.

Number of Horse.

1st. The *Bhungee Misul*, at the head of which were the chiefs HUREE SINGH, JHUNDA SINGH and GHUNDA SINGH, originally three Jât cultivators of the Dooab. The Misul derived its name from the extraordinary addiction of its members to the use of *Bhung*, an intoxicating smoking material, prepared from the leaves of the Hemp plant. Its possessions are now incorporated in the Lahôr dominions, ... 10,000

2nd. The *Ramgurheea Misul*, taking its name from a village east of Lahôr, of which the chief, JUSA SINGH, was originally a *Thoka* or carpenter. Its possessions are also incorporated in RUNJEET SINGH's dominions, ... 3,000

3rd. The *Ghunneya Misul*, headed by JY SINGH, a Jât of Ghunnee, which lies also east of Lahôr. Its possessions have likewise been seized by RUNJEET SINGH, ... 8,000

4th. The *Nukeea Misul,* deriving its name from Nukee, a tract of country lying south-west of Lahôr, and bordering on Mooltan. It had several leaders, all Jât cultivators, of low extraction. Its possessions have been seized, and it no longer exists as a separate body,.......... 2,000

5th. The *Aloowala Misul,* headed then by JUSA SINGH, *Kulal,* or mace-bearer, who rose to great eminence amongst the Sikhs, and by his followers was honored with the title of Badshah. His possessions lay on both sides of the Sutlej, and the present chief, a descendant of JUSA SINGH, holds those to the east under British protection. He is a grandee of the Court of RUNJEET SINGH, treated with distinction, but subject to continual exactions on account of his Punjab territory,................................ 3,000

6th. The *Duleeala Misul,* headed by TARA SINGH GHYBA, a shepherd of Dulee, a village on the Ravee, east of Lahôr, who received the nickname of GHYBA, from his ingenious devices for conveying goats and lambs across the torrents to feed. TARA SINGH'S possessions are incorporated in RUNJEET SINGH'S dominions, but the Roopur, and some other Sirdars of the Misul, having possessions east of the Sutlej, are under British protection,.......................... 7,500

7th. The *Nishan-wala Misul,* headed by SUNGUT SINGH and MOHUR SINGH, the standard bearers of the Dul, or assembled Sikh army, whence the name was derived. The families of both chiefs are extinct, and Umbala, one of its possessions, lapsed in consequence to the British: Shahabad belonging to subordinate chiefs, is under protection, ... 12,000

8th. The *Fyzoollapoorea Misul,* sometimes styled *Singhpoorea,* headed by KUPOOR SINGH and KHOOSHHAL SINGH, of Fyzoollapoor, a village near Umritsur, the Mohummedan name of which the Sikhs changed to Singhpoor. The chiefs were Jât Zemindars, KUPOOR SINGH was styled Nuwab by his followers; their possessions west of the Sutlej, have been seized, but those to the east are still held by their descendants under British protection,.......................... 2,500

9th. The *Krora-Singhea Misul,* headed by KRORA SINGH, and afterwards by BHUGAEEL SINGH, both Jâts. KRORA SINGH left no heir. BHUGAEEL SINGH'S possessions in the Punjab have been absorbed, but his widow holds Chiloundee and 22 other villages east of the Sutlej, under British protection. Chicheroulee belonging to a subordinate chief of the Misul, is also under protection, and Bhudâwur has lasped, ... 12,000

10th. The *Shuheed* and *Nihung Misul,* headed by KURUM SINGH and GOOR BUKSH SINGH. The name which signifies Martyrs, was acquired by the first chiefs, ancestors of those named, who were beheaded by the Mohummedans at Dumduma, west of Puteeala. Their possessions lie east of the Sutlej, and are protected, ... 2,000

11th. The *Phoolkea* and *Bhykea Misul*, headed by Raja ALA SINGH, and afterwards by Raja UMUR SINGH, his grandson, of Puteeala. Phool was the Jât progenitor of the Puteeala, Nabah, Jeend, and Kythul chiefs, all of whom are under British protection, ... 5,000

12th. The *Sookur-Chukea Misul*, headed by CHURUT SINGH, ancestor of RUNJEET SINGH, the present sovereign of Lahôr, whose progenitors were Jât Zumeendars of Sookur-Chuk, ... 2,500

69,500

In the above list the Misul of CHURUT SINGH holds the last place, and was formed probably after the successful defence of Gujraolee, and the defeat of KHAJA OBYD had raised the reputation, and given a new distinction to that chief. Every Misul acted independently, or in concert, as necessity or inclination suggested, but there was generally an assembly of the chiefs called the *Surhut Khalsa*, held twice a year at Umritsur during the Bysakhee and Dewalee festivals, which occur in April and October. On these occasions, after bathing in the sacred reservoir, they generally held a *Goormutta*, or special council, where expeditions of importance, or any matters of more than ordinary moment were submitted to their united wisdom. If the joint forces of several Misuls took the field upon any predatory enterprize, or to collect *Rakha* (Black Mail), the army assumed the denomination of a *Dul* of the *Khalsa Jee*.

When the Misuls acquired their territorial possessions, it became the first duty of the chiefs to partition out the lands, towns, and villages amongst those who considered themselves as having made the conquest, *Shamil*, or in common. Every *Surkunda*, or leader of the smallest party of horse that fought under the standard of the Misul, demanded his share, in proportion to the degree in which he had contributed to the acquisition, and, as they received no pay from the chief, and he had no other recompense to offer for their services, there was no resource but to adopt this mode of satisfying them. The *sirdaree* or chief's portion being first divided off, the remainder was separated into *Puttees* or parcels for each Surkunda, and these were again subdivided and parcelled out to inferior leaders, according to the number of horse they brought into the field. Each took his portion as a co-sharer, and held it in absolute independence.

It was impossible that this state of things should subsist long in the Punjab, any more than it had done in England, France, and other countries of Europe, when they similarly fell a prey to hordes of associated warriors, who acknowledged no systematic general authority or government. When the link of a common enemy and common danger was removed, and the chiefs were converted from needy adventurers to lords of domains, discords and mutual plunderings commenced, as temper, ambition, or avarice, excited to contention. Cause of quarrel was never wanting in the confusion of the coparcenary system. The disputes and divisions which subsisted in each lordship, favoured the designs of the aspiring from without, whose aid being solicited by one of the parties, an opening was frequently found to eject both. In cases of frontier disputes, or of injury, or wrong of any kind sustained or fancied, the chief would call upon his kindred and retainers to furnish him the means of redress, and they would feel bound by a sense of honor not to fail, when the *Chara*, or gathering was demanded in such a cause; but in a matter of internal strife within the Misul, every one would be free to choose his own side, and either party would deem it fair to fortify itself with any aid it could command from without. Upon occasions of gathering, it became customary for the chief, or person demanding it, to pay a rupee per *kathee* or saddle; in other respects, the service was gratuitous, and plunder was the reward expected by those who joined either standard. The past life and habits of the Sikhs precluded any scruples on their part as to the conduct or character of their associates. The most daring culprits found ready admission into their ranks, and it was a point of honor to deliver no one upon demand of a neighbour, whatever might be the crime laid to his charge. Hence arose the practise of *Gaha*, or self-redress, by individuals, no less than by chiefs; and every owner of a village was compelled to surround his possession with a wall and ditch, while in towns, or places held in joint property, the houses of the coparcenary, and of all who were exposed to the appetence or revengeful passions of others, were built as towers or keeps, and a fort in joint tenancy would ordinarily be divided by an inner retrenchment, as a protection against treachery from the fellow occupant.

The tenure that has been described above is the *Puteedaree*, that of every associate in the Misul of less rank than a Sirdar, down even to the single horseman, who equipped and mounted himself: all these regulated entirely the management of their *putee*, fining, confining, or even further illtreating, according to their pleasure, any Zumeendar, or working Ryot of their allotment. His complaint could not be listened to or redressed by any superior ; but in case of quarrel with an equal, reference would be made to the Surkunda, and if his decision failed to give satisfaction, an appeal might be made to the general Sirdar. The more ordinary mode, however, was to collect friends and relations, and seek a prompt self-redress. It was not legitimate for a Puteedar to sell his tenure to a stranger, but he might mortgage it to satisfy any present want, and at his demise might settle by will, to which of his male relations it should go. Reciprocal aid for mutual protection and defence, was the relation on which a Puteedar stood in other respects to the Sirdar, and the only condition of his tenure.

Besides the Puteedaree, however, there were three other tenures created, arising out of the circumstances, in which different chiefs found themselves, from the manner of their association with those who composed their Misul. These were the *Misuldaree*, the *Tabadaree* and the *Jageerdaree*.

Bodies of inferior strength, or petty chiefs with their followers, attached themselves sometimes to a Misul, without subscribing to any conditions of association or dependence. The allotments of land assigned to such, would be considered as the free reward of their co-operation, and would be held in no sort of dependence ; they were called Misuldaree. If dissatisfied with his chief a Misuldar might transfer himself with his possessions to another, under whose protection or countenance he might prefer to continue.

A *Tâbadar* was on the other hand a retainer, as the word is understood in Europe, one completely subservient; the lands which were his reward, were liable to forfeiture for any act of disobedience or rebellion, and at the caprice of the Sirdar might be resumed upon any occasion of displeasure.

The third class of tenures or *Jageers* were given to needy relations, dependents, and entertained soldiers who deserved well, and the holders were liable to be called upon for their personal services at all times, with their quotas or contingents, equipped and mounted at their own charge, according to the extent of the grant. These were even further under the power of the Sirdar than the Tâbadaree grants. Both were hereditary only according to his pleasure, the lands of them formed part of the allotment set apart for the Sirdaree, and the Misul, or association, had, of course, nothing to say in such assignments.

The religious and charitable appropriations and grants, viz, those made to Sikh Gooroos, Soodees, and Baidees, or to endowments for temples, and for charitable distributions of alms, and sometimes even to Moosulman Peerzadas, need no description, for they had nothing to distinguish them from what are found all over India.

The above explanation has been necessary to give some idea of the state of things, which resulted from the two provinces of Lahôr and Sirhind being left to be occupied by the Sikhs, when, finally abandoned by the Afghans, as they had previously been by the Moghul and Dehlee officers. The European reader will at once be struck by the similarity between the condition of things above described, and the relations which have been handed down to us of what occurred in England, when the Saxons similarly spread and occupied that country; and when Clovis and the Franks seized the fairest portion of Gaul. The arrangements for government were the very rudest that the most ignorant tribes ever devised: and, though the ideologist may find something attractive in contemplating such attempts to realize in practise the dream of universal independence and equality of condition between individuals, he must, indeed, be a bold speculator in politics, who would assume that any class could find happiness, contentment, or rest, in a country ruled by seventy thousand sovereigns, as were the unfortunate provinces of Lahôr and Sirhind, when the Sikhs assumed dominion over them.

CHAPTER THIRD.

A. D. 1773 to 1791.

Feuds and contentions of the Sikhs. Rise and fall of different chiefs. The history of Churut Singh and Maha Singh, ancestors of Runjeet Singh, traced to the death of the latter, and Runjeet's assumption of the direction of affairs.

In resuming the progress of events in the Punjab, the narrator has henceforward only to record the squabbles and petty feuds, which arose amongst the chiefs thus left in possession, and as these ordinarily were of little interest and less variety, those only deserve relation, which contributed to produce the status now observed, in other words, those in which the ancestors of RUNJEET SINGH, or himself, bore a part.

The hill Raja of Jummoo, RUNJEET DEO by name, had a misunderstanding with his eldest son BRIJ-RAJ, and desired to set aside his pretensions to the succession in favour of the youngest, MEEAN DULEL SINGH. In order to secure his hereditary rights, BRIJ-RAJ broke into rebellion, and applied to CHURUT SINGH, offering a large yearly tribute on condition of his aiding to effect the deposition of his father. CHURUT SINGH having an old enmity against RUNJEET DEO, closed with the offer, and strengthening himself by association with JY SINGH of the Ghuneea Misul, their united force marched into the hills and encamped at Oodhachur, on the bank of the Busuntee river. The Raja having received timely notice of the designs of the heir-apparent, had made corresponding preparations for resistance. The defence of the capital he reserved to himself, but collected a force to oppose the invasion, composed of auxiliaries from Chumba, Noorpoor, Busehur, and Kangra, in the hills, to which were added, besides a party of his own troops, the confederated forces of the Bhungee Misul under JHUNDA SINGH, whom he induced to lend his services in the extremity. The two armies lay encamped on opposite sides of the Busuntee, and in a partial skirmish between the Sikh auxiliaries CHURUT SINGH was killed by the bursting of his own matchlock.

He was 45 years of age, and had risen from a common Dharwee or highwayman, to be Sirdar of a separate Misul, with a territory computed to yield about three lakhs of rupees. He left a widow, DESAN by name, with two sons and a daughter, called respectively MAHA SINGH, SUHUJ SINGH and RAJ KOONWUR. The eldest son MAHA SINGH, then ten years of age, succeeded to the Sirdaree, but the widow and JY SINGH Ghunee assumed the immediate direction of affairs. It was determined by them to assassinate JHUNDA SINGH Bhungee, who was the main stay of the Jummoo Raja's party, and the avowed enemy of both the Sookur-Chukeea and Ghunee Misuls. A sweeper was tempted by a large bribe, to undertake this hazardous enterprize, and he succeeded in effecting his purpose by firing at and mortally wounding the Bhungee chief, as he was walking unattended through the Jummoo camp. The Sookurchukeea and Ghunee Sikhs being satisfied with the revenge thus taken, withdrew soon after from the enterprize in which they had engaged. The Bhungee troops had similarly left the opposite camp on the death of their chief. Thus BRIJ-RAJ DEO was left alone to settle with his father his rights of inheritance to the Raj: before the departure, however, of MAHA SINGH, he went through the ceremony of an exchange of turbands (*Dustarbudlee,*) with BRIJ-RAJ, which bound him to brotherhood for life. These events occurred in 1774.*

Several subordinate Sirdars of CHURUT SINGH'S recently formed Misul, mistrusting the youth of MAHA SINGH, or dissatisfied with the Regent widow, aimed now to shake off their dependence. Of these, one DHURUM SINGH was the first to commit himself by an overt act of rebellion. He relied on the succour and countenance of GHUNDA SINGH, JHUNDA SINGH'S successor, in the Sirdaree of the Bhungee Misul, but was deceived in his expectations, and suffered forfeiture of his lands for contumacy, before any aid could come to his relief. The rest

* Captain WADE gives 1771 as the date of CHURUT SINGH'S death, and states it to have occurred in a general action with the Bhungee Sikhs at Suhawara, near Jusar Dodeh, in the Rich,hua Dooab. He concurs in assigning the bursting of his matchlock as the cause of CHURUT SINGH'S death, but says that JHUNDA SINGH was shot by a man of his own party in the course of the action. The discrepance, except that of date, is not very material; but it is singular that such an event should be so differently reported to the two officers—Captain MURRAY is deemed the superior authority, and his version has therefore been adhered to. In like manner, Captain WADE differs from Captain MURRAY in the date assigned to the birth of MAHA SINGH. Captain W. places it in 1757, making him 14 years old in 1771, when CHURUT SINGH died according to his version. Captain MURRAY fixes it in 1764, making him 10 years old in 1774.

were deterred by this example, and the moment appearing favorable, the nuptials of MAHA SINGH were celebrated in 1776, with the daughter of GUJPUT SINGH, of Jeend, to whom he had previously been betrothed. JY SINGH and a large armed force of Sookurchukea and Ghunee Sikhs crossed the Sutlej with the *Burât* to Budrookh, where the young chief was met by his bride; and a large concourse of Sirdars of the nation did honor to the ceremony, it being with them obligatory to give attendance on such occasions, and the omission being looked upon as a slight and a wide deviation from propriety.

MAHA SINGH is next heard of as the associate of JY SINGH in an enterprize for the capture of Rusool-Nugur, now called Ram-Nugur by the Sikhs, situated on the east bank of the Chunab, and held by a Jât Moosulman, named PEER MOHUMMED, who was at the head of the ancient tribe of *Chutta*, styled sometimes *Munchureea*, from a considerable town in their occupation, and many of whom have embraced the religion of the Koran. The pretext for this attack was, that the tribe had given up to the *Bhungee Misul* a large piece of ordnance, left behind by the Abdalee Shah, and placed with them in deposit, from inability to cross it over the Chunab. This gun was of much celebrity, and is now known as the *Bhungee Top:* it was claimed for the *Khalsa* or Sikh nation at large, to be appropriated by an assembly of chiefs. Rusool Nugur was besieged and blockaded for four months, and the Bhungee Sikhs being employed at the time in plundering and seeking possessions, or in levying tribute in the Mooltan and Buhawulpoor districts, neglected to afford succour or relief. The place consequently fell to MAHA SINGH, who acquired great reputation by this early feat of arms, so much so, that many independent Sirdars, who had hitherto attached themselves to the Bhungee Misul, transferred their services and preferred to follow his leading in war, and to live under his countenance and protection.

Two years after this event, on the 2d November 1780, a son was born to MAHA SINGH, by his wife, of the Jeend family, and named RUNJEET SINGH. The child was attacked by the small-pox at a very early age, and the disease taking an unfavorable turn, his life was endangered, whereupon the father, according to Asiatic custom, made large donations to the poor in charity, fed multitudes of Brahmins and holy men to secure their prayers, and sent gifts to the sacred temples at Kangra and Juwala-Mookhee. The boy recovered, but with the loss of one of his eyes, whence he is termed *Kana*, or the one-eyed; and his face in other respects is marked with the disease. MAHA SINGH was engaged at this period in settling the territory he had inherited or acquired, and in extending his influence and connexions. The *Bhungees* lost their principal Sirdars, and having aimed to establish themselves in Mooltan, brought down on themselves an Afghan army, which retook the city from them, and further ejected them from Buhawulpoor and Munkera. The consequence was, that the power of the Misul was effectually broken, and the rising fortune and reputation of MAHA SINGH enabled him to extend his relations and strengthen himself from its ruin. He was cautious, however, of engaging in any direct hostility with his Sikh brethren, well knowing that to follow such means of aggrandizement, would breed ill will, and lead probably to a confederacy, and gathering for his destruction.

Again, the Afghan power was still too formidable, and too united, for him to hope to aggrandize himself at the expense of that nation. His restless spirit was, however, not long in finding a quarter in which to pursue his schemes at pleasure.

Raja RUNJEET DEO of Jummoo was dead, and his son BRIJ-RAJ DEO having succeeded to that Raj, proved unworthy and debauched, so that discontent prevailed in the principality, and afforded an opening for interference. MAHA SINGH tempted by this state of things, resolved to exact tribute, and enforce fealty from his turband brother; he accordingly moved with a force into the hills, and BRIJ-RAJ being in no condition for resistance, fled to the Trikota-Devee mountain, a three-peaked eminence, where is an *Usthan* or temple of Bishun-Devee, in which the Hindoo Devotee presents an offering of cocoanuts, deemed more agreeable to the benevolent goddess than the heads of goats. The town of Jummoo was at this period very prosperous and rich, for, in consequence of the distractions of the Punjab, many of the wealthy merchants had been induced to seek an asylum, or to establish a branch-firm within the hills beyond their influence. Jummoo was well situated for this purpose, while under RUNJEET DEO the resort of this class of persons to his dominions was encouraged, and they lived in ease and security. MAHA SINGH and his Sikhs sacked the town, and ravaged the whole territory of Jummoo, and he is reported to have brought away a large spoil, including much specie and valuables of all kinds.

By this conduct MAHA SINGH, though he enriched himself, raised also many enemies. The Bhungee Sikhs who had long maintained a connexion with Jummoo, were highly irritated, and, what was even of more consequence to MAHA SINGH'S rising fortunes, the displeasure and jealousy of his old Mentor and guardian, JY SINGH, of Ghunee, was incurred. This chief was now in the zenith of his power, and was of a haughty imperious temper. MAHA SINGH on his return from the hills proceeded with his booty to Umritsur, with the double purpose of paying his respects to JY SINGH, and performing his ablutions in the holy reservoir. The old chief received him with marked coolness and displeasure, so much so that MAHA SINGH assuming the demeanour of an inferior, approached with a tray of sweetmeats in his hand, and begged to be made acquainted with the cause he had given for offence, professing his sense of filial obligation and attachment to JY SINGH, and offering any atonement in his power. JY SINGH was stretched at length on his couch, and, drawing his sheet over him, called out loudly and rudely, that he desired to hear no more of the Bhugtea's (dancing boy's) pathetic conversation. MAHA SINGH retired in high indignation at this reception, and determined to be revenged for the insult. He mounted his horse, and, with a few followers, made his escape secretly from Umritsur, where JY SINGH'S power and influence were paramount, and returned to his home to seek the means of executing his purposes. Being too weak to enter the field against the *Ghunee* and *Bhungee Misuls* alone, he cast about for associates, and determined to make a friend of JUSA SINGH, Sirdar of the Ramghureea Misul, who had recently been ousted from his possessions in the Punjab by a confederacy of the Aloowala and Ghunee associations, and the latter had been considerable gainers by the aggression. Agents were immediately dispatched to recall JUSA SINGH, and to assure him of aid and support, if disposed to make an effort for the recovery of his lost possessions. The despoiled chief was living by depredations in the Dooab of the Jumna and Ganges, with the wilds of Hansee and Hisar for his place of refuge; having satisfied himself of the motives of MAHA SINGH'S offer, and being convinced that it was sincere, he lost no time in returning into the Punjab, with all the force he could collect.

The combined troops of MAHA SINGH and JUSA SINGH now appeared suddenly within a few miles of Battala, the principal town of JY SINGH'S possessions, and where he had fixed his residence. Here they were joined by SUNSAR CHUND, Raja of Kôt Kangra in the hills, and by UMUR SINGH BUGREH, and some other disaffected tributaries of the Ghunee Sirdar, who had been stirred up by MAHA SINGH. JY SINGH was now called upon to render up the share of the Ramghureea possessions, which had been allotted to him, and, on his refusal, the invaders proceeded to occupy and ravage the country. JY SINGH made a gathering of his Misul, and placing his son GOOR BUKHSH SINGH at the head of 8000 horse, sent him to punish and expel the invaders. An action ensued, in which GOOR BUKHSH exposed himself with youthful rashness, and was slain; whereupon his followers dispersed and fled, and the victors soon after made themselves masters of Battala, when JY SINGH being humbled, was compelled to sue for peace. It was granted to him by the young chief he had insulted, under condition that he should render up the Ramghureea lands to JUSA SINGH, and the fort of Kangra, which he had obtained by stratagem, to SUNSAR CHUND. These terms being accepted, the allies retained the town of Battala, but towards the close of the year SUDA KOONWUR, widow of GOOR BUKHSH SINGH succeeded by intrigue with the inhabitants in ejecting the garrison and recovering it.

JY SINGH had set his hopes on the promise afforded by the character of GOOR BUKHSH; and though he had two other sons, by name BAGH SINGH and NIDHAN SINGH, he treated them with neglect, his whole affections being engrossed by the family of his deceased son. The widow, SUDA KOONWUR, had paramount influence, and gained an entire ascendant over the old man, and as she was of an aspiring, bold spirit, she procured that a separate appanage of some villages about Sohnan and Hajeepoor should be set apart for the surviving sons, while she regulated every thing at Battala for the interest of herself and her only child by GOOR BUKHSH, a daughter. At her suggestion, a negociation was opened for the affiance of the girl, whose name was MEHTAB-KOONWUR, to RUNJEET SINGH, the young son of MAHA SINGH, whom she hoped thus to bind to a permanent reconciliation, and through his friendship and powerful support to secure for herself the Sirdaree upon her father-in-law's decease. MAHA SINGH assented readily to the union, and the *Mungnee*, or betrothment, of the children was duly performed in the year 1785, and contributed further to raise MAHA SINGH in power and reputation; for through the friendship of the Ramghureea Sirdar, and Kangra Raja, which was permanently secured by his aid in the recovery of their lost possessions, added to the influence resulting from this close connexion with the Ghunee Misul, there was no one in the Punjab, or of the Sikh nation, that could compete with him in authority, or command equal means if called upon for an exertion. The result was favorable to the prosperity of the country, and the Punjab for several years during this chief's ascendancy, enjoyed a repose and tranquillity to which it had long been a stranger.

Until 1791 MAHA SINGH continued to administer in peace the territory he had acquired, and to exercise his influence for the benefit of those connected with him. In that year GOOJUR SINGH, the Sikh chief of Goojrat, died, and SAHEB SINGH, his son, succeeded to the Sirdaree. The sister of MAHA SINGH had been given in marriage to SAHEB SINGH by CHURUT SINGH, but the ties of affinity had little influence in restraining ambitious views, and the desire of aggrandizement which filled the mind of MAHA SINGH, was not to be so checked. He deemed the moment favorable for asserting superiority over Goojrat, and for claiming tribute. SAHEB SINGH evaded compliance, alleging that his father was an adherent of the Bhungee Misul, and had never fought under the standard of the Sookurchukeea, to whom he acknowledged no dependance. MAHA SINGH marched on receiving this reply and besieged SAHEB SINGH in his fort of Soo[illegible]. The Goojrateea chief applied in his distress to the Bhungee Sikhs, and KURUM SINGH DOOLOO came with the strength of that Misul to interrupt the siege. Though not strong enough to enter the field with MAHA SINGH, they hovered about his camp, and put him to considerable inconvenience for supplies; a detachment of the Sookurchukeeas however succeeded after a time in beating up the quarters and plundering the camp of the Bhungees, after which the siege proceeded. MAHA SINGH had been three months before the place, when in the early part of the year 1792 he became seriously ill. The siege was immediately broken up, and the chief being carried back to his principal place of residence Goojraolee, expired there in the twenty-seventh year of his age. He was brave, active, and prudent beyond his years, and left a high reputation amongst his nation, for all the qualities of a Sirdar. He shook off the trammels of his mother's guardianship at the early age of seventeen, and some time after, having detected her in an intrigue with a Brahmin, put her to death with his own hand; an act of barbarous justice, that does not seem to have lessened his reputation, or in any way to have affected his character injuriously in the eyes of his cotemporaries.

MAHA SINGH left only one son, the present RUNJEET SINGH, who was then in his twelfth year. His mother became regent, and was assisted by the minister of her husband, LUKHOO or LUKHPUT SINGH. SUDA KOONWUR, the minor chief's mother-in-law, exerted also much influence in the conduct of affairs, and in the year following, viz. in 1793, the demise of JY SINGH left the Ghunee Misul likewise under her direction, every thing having been prepared before hand, for the exclusion of the sons of that Sirdar.

Little care was taken of the education of RUNJEET SINGH: the means were furnished to him of gratifying every youthful passion or desire, and his early years were passed in indulgence and in following the sports of the field. He was never taught to read or write in any language. While still in tutelage, however, a second marriage was contracted for him with RAJ KOONWUR, a daughter of the Nukee chief, KHUJAN SINGH.

Upon attaining the age of 17 years, RUNJEET SINGH, in imitation of his father, assumed in person the conduct of affairs, and dismissed the Dewan: it is further stated that, under the guidance of DUL SINGH, his father's maternal uncle, who had long borne ill-will to the Dewan, LUKHOO was dispatched on an expedition to Kitas, where he was slain in an affray with the Zumeendars, not without suspicions of contrivance. His father's example gave sanction to an act of further cruelty in RUNJEET SINGH. The regent mother was accused of having led a life of profligate indulgence, the late Dewan being not the only paramour admitted to her favors. Upon receiving evidence to this, it is said, that RUNJEET SINGH gave his sanction to, or at least connived at, her being put to death, and the old chief, DUL SINGH, is designated as the perpetrator of the act by means of poison.* RUNJEET SINGH, with the advice of SUDA KOONWUR, carried on now in person all the affairs of his Sirdaree, and the difficulties he experienced, with the means by which he extricated himself, and made every circumstance contribute to his further rise, will form the subject of the Chapters which follow.

* The above particulars are from Captain WADE's Report. Captain MURRAY merely states, that "he dismissed the Dewan, and caused his mother to be assassinated." Captain WADE assigns the year 1787 for the decease of MAHA SINGH, and states him to have been born in 1757, as before remarked, which are discrepancies of date with Captain MURRAY, for which I am unable to account; the latter is the authority followed.

CHAPTER FOURTH.

A. D. 1794 to 1808.

The early administration of Runjeet Singh. His aggrandizement at the expense of other Sikh Sirdars, to his treaty with the British Government, and exclusion from the countries east of the Sutlej.

In the course of the years 1795, 1796, and 1797, the Punjab was twice exposed to invasion by Shah Zuman, who had recently succeeded the peaceful Tymoor on the throne of Kabool. The Sikhs ventured not to oppose him openly in the field, and his coming, therefore, was a source of infinite confusion, leading to a temporary abandonment of their possessions by the Sirdars near his route. In 1798 the Shah advanced again, and entered Lahôr, without opposition; but, after a few months stay there, finding it impossible to make any arrangements for the permanent occupation of the country, or to render the Punjab in other respects a source of advantage to himself, he retraced his steps to his hereditary dominions west of the Indus, and the Sikh Sirdars returned each to the territory he had acquired, and which had been evacuated on the Shah's approach. RUNJEET SINGH was one of those who retired before the Shah, and on this last occasion he joined other Sirdars similarly circumstanced with himself, or otherwise linked to his Misul, and made an expedition across the Sutlej, where he employed the interval of the Shah's stay at Lahôr in a tour for the exaction of tribute, and for the reduction to his authority of any towns or villages he could master.

Upon the retirement of the Shah, RUNJEET SINGH began to entertain designs for securing Lahôr to himself, and his mother-in-law, SUDA KOONWUR, encouraged and lent her aid to forward his views. The city was at this time in the joint possession of CHYT SINGH, MOHUR SINGH, and SAHEB SINGH. RUNJEET SINGH, however, by an opportune service to ZUMAN SHAH, obtained from that prince a grant with permission to take possession. The Afghan had been compelled to precipitate his retreat from the Punjab, by intelligence of designs from Persia on the side of Herat, having for their object the support of the claims of SHAH MAHMOOD. On arriving at the Jhilem, that river was found swollen with temporary rain, so that the Afghan artillery could not be crossed. Not thinking it expedient to wait on this account, SHAH ZUMAN wrote to RUNJEET SINGH, to extricate and forward to him the guns left behind, holding out the hope, that his known wishes in respect to Lahôr might be complied with, if this duty were well performed. The politic Sikh raised eight out of the twelve guns, from the bed of the river into which they had sunk, and forwarded them to the Shah, from whom he received in return the grant he desired. The remaining four guns were raised only in 1823, and are now in the arsenal at Lahôr*.

Armed with this authority as an influence over the Mohummedan population of the town, and assisted by the credit and troops of SUDA KOONWUR, RUNJEET SINGH prepared an expedition for the seizure of the city of Lahôr. The three Sikh chiefs in possession were shameless in conduct, profligate and debauched, and neglectful of the means of securing themselves. They had few troops or retainers, and their administration was most unpopular. In order to prepare the way for the success of his scheme, RUNJEET SINGH deputed KAZEE UBDOOR-RUHMAN, a native of Rusoolnugur, to open an intrigue with some of the principal Moosulman inhabitants. MEER MOHKUM, manager for CHYT SINGH, with MOHUMMUD ASHIK and MEER SHADEE, were won over to assist the project, and promised on the approach of RUNJEET SINGH, to open one of the gates to him; accordingly he marched, accompanied by his mother-in-law, and, having been admitted without opposition, CHYT SINGH and his two co-partners, were compelled to accept Jageers for subsistence; and RUNJEET SINGH thus established his own authority, and made arrangements to secure his conquest. His successful aggression and acquisition of a place so famous excited the jealousy of all rival Sirdars, and an assembly of troops for recovery of this city took place at Basim. GOOLAB SINGH Bhungee, SAHEB SINGH of Goojrat, and NUJUM-OOD-DEEN of Kasoor, were the chiefs at the head of

* The fact of RUNJEET SING's having obtained a grant of Lahôr from the Afghan Sovereign, is not mentioned by Captain MURRAY. The statement, with the circumstances under which it was alleged to be procured, is made on the authority of Captain WADE.

the confederacy most active in hostility to RUNJEET SINGH. After a few months of debate however, and some fruitless skirmishes, finding the young chief well prepared, their army broke up, and the city was left ever after in RUNJEET SINGH's uninterrupted possession.

The Moosulmans of Kasoor, a considerable town, stated to be about 25 kôs S. E. of Lahôr, incurred the just resentment of RUNJEET SINGH, as well by the part their chief had taken in this confederacy, as by depredations since committed by them up to the gates of the city. His next enterprize was against their possessions, and in 1801-2 NUJUM-OOD-DEEN was compelled to submit to terms, binding himself to furnish a quota of troops under his brother KOOTUB-OOD-DEEN, and to become a feudatory of RUNJEET SINGH. In the same year the young chief, having proceeded to bathe in the sacred reservoir of Gooroo Ram-Das at Tarun-Turun, met there Sirdar FUTEH SINGH, of the Aloowala Misul, and contracting a friendship with him, made an exchange of turbands.

The year 1802 was marked by the birth* of KHURUK SINGH, the present heir-apparent of MAHA RAJA RUNJEET SINGH: his mother was RAJ-KOONWUR, daughter of KHUJAN SINGH of Nukee. In the same year, the fort of Cheniot held by JUSA SINGH, son of the Bhungee chief, KURUM SINGH DOOLOO, was besieged, and, after a short resistance, taken by RUNJEET SINGH, who made to the expelled chief a trifling allowance for maintenance.

* Captain WADE places this event after the decease of DUL SINGH, and pending measures to occupy his Jageer and fort of Aleepoor, which, according to Captain MURRAY, would make it in 1804. The year 1802, is, however, assigned as the date by both Officers.

In the month of December 1802, RUNJEET SINGH assembled his own and SUDA KOONWUR'S forces, and being joined by the Aloowala, the three united Misuls fell suddenly on the family of GOOLAB SINGH, the last Bhungee Sirdar of note, who had been always at feud with MAHA SINGH when living, and was at the head of the confederacy which had attempted to recover Lahôr. GOOLAB SINGH had died in 1800, leaving a widow named RANEE SOOKHA, and a son GOORDUT SINGH, still a minor, under her guardianship. The moment was considered favorable to break for ever the power of the Bhungees. Accordingly, the widow was called upon to surrender the fort of Lohgurh in Umritsur, to give up the great Bhungee gun, and in other respects to submit to the confederates. Feeling unequal to resist, the helpless widow evacuated Lohgurh, and fled with her child, and the family has since sunk to indigence and obscurity.

Pending this operation, a domestic feud occurred in Kasoor; and, NUJUM-OOD-DEEN being assassinated, was succeeded in the Sirdaree, by KOOTUB-OOD-DEEN, his brother. The juncture appearing favorable, RUNJEET SINGH moved down, with a large force of confederated Sikhs against that territory, but after plundering the open country for three months, finding he could make no impression on the strong holds which are numerous in the district, he accepted a pecuniary payment, and retired. In March of this year, Raja SUNSAR CHUND, of Kôt Kangra, in the hills, made a descent into the plains and plundered some villages in the territory of SUDA KOONWUR, that is, belonging to the Ghunee Misul. She called for the aid of her son-in-law, who marched immediately with FUTEH SINGH ALOOWALA, and soon expelled the mountaineers. The occasion was taken to invest Soojanpoor, which was held by the Sikh chief BOODH SINGH BHUGUT, from whom a sum of ready money, a large piece of ordnance, and the three districts of Buhrampoor, Dhurumkot, and Sookhalgurh, were extorted.

From the Jalundhur Dooab, where these operations had carried him, RUNJEET SINGH crossed the Ravee, and returned to Lahôr by a detour through Sealkot and Rusoolnugur, plundering as he went. The widow of CHOOR-MUL was, during this march, deprived of Phugwara, which was given in an exchange to FUTEH SINGH ALOOWALA. SUNSAR CHUND ventured again into the plains towards the close of the year, and seized several towns in the Jalundhur, but decamped again on the march thither of RUNJEET with a body of Aloowala and Ghunee confederates. In February following, the Hill Raja again appeared, and having seized Hoshyarpoor and Bijwara, attempted to maintain himself there. From both, however, he was expelled by the Sikhs, and RUNJEET SINGH, after this service, made a tour of exaction, in which, either as gift or tribute, he obtained considerable sums from the old Sikh chiefs, TARA SINGH GHYBA, DHURUM SINGH, of Umritsur, and BOODH SINGH, of Fyzoollapoor. His conduct excited the jealousy and fears of all the Sirdars, who had hitherto enjoyed independence, and immunity from molestation. They saw that RUNJEET aimed to reduce them to fealty and subservience; yet were they so divided, and filled with jealousies, and without a head or leader, that they attempted nothing, and could devise no scheme to relieve themselves from his arbitrary exactions, and from the forfeiture and resumption with which he seemed systematically to visit the family of every chief that died. It was in this year that DUL SINGH, the brother-in-law of CHURUT SINGH, died, when RUNJEET acquired Akulgurh* and Jummabad by escheat, these places being held as dependencies of the Sookurchukea Misul. DUL SINGH had been in disgrace some time before his death.

The dissensions of the four sons of TYMOOR SHAH, HUMAYOON, MUHMOOD, SHAH ZUMAN, and SHAH SHOOJAH, began at this time to produce distractions in the Afghan empire, which led to the royal authority being every where held in contempt. RUNJEET SINGH was encouraged by this state of things to direct his views westward, and after a Dusera, passed in more than ordinary excess at Lahôr, he determined in the year 1804 to seek further aggrandizement by the seizure of the dependencies of that empire, east of the Indus. He accordingly crossed the Ravee in October; and, having the Aloowala chief in attendance, moved to Ramnugur on the Chunab, and thence to Jhung, held by AHMED KHAN, a chief of considerable note. The Khan made his submission, and bought off the invaders. Saheewal and Kot Maharaja, possessions of two Balooch Moosulmans, were next visited, and an acknowledgment of supremacy with presents of horses and other gifts, saved them from ravage. As the season advanced preparation was made to visit the neighbourhood of Mooltan, but the governor MOZUFFUR KHAN anticipated the design, and averted the evil from his subjects and dependents by the transmission of timely and rich presents. Relations were then established with all the Moosulman chiefs and

* Formerly Aleepoor, a possession of the Chitta Moosulmans. The name was changed by the Sikhs on their capturing the place in 1770.

families settled about the Chunab and Jhylum; and, although the amount obtained in this first visit in the way of tribute, or by gifts, was not large, the effect of the operations of the season was beneficial for the ulterior views of the aspiring Sikh, for the chiefs, as far as the Indus, began to see to what quarter their hopes and fears must thenceforward be directed: most of them at once made their election for submission to the ruler of Lahôr, and withdrew from this period from further connexion with the Kabool court or its officers.

In February 1805 RUNJEET SINGH returned to his capital, which was now established at Lahôr, and celebrating there the Hoolee Saturnalia, he went afterwards with a slight attendance to the annual fair held at the time of performing ablutions in the Ganges at Hurdwar. The ceremonies of his religion being there completed, he returned towards the beginning of June, and employed the rains in farming out the revenues of the districts retained in his personal administration to the highest bidders. This has ever been his only scheme of revenue management. The farmer has full powers even of life and death over those committed to his tender mercies, and his lease is a mere licence to rob.

After the Dusera of 1805, the Sikh army was again led by RUNJEET SINGH into the Mohummedan Territory between the Chunab and Indus, and the chief of Jhung was called upon to settle for an annual tribute, the demand upon him being now raised to 120,000 rupees. Before however this negociation could be brought to a conclusion, RUNJEET SINGH was recalled by intelligence of the near approach of JUSWUNT RAO HOLKUR and AMEER KHAN from the east, pursued by the British army under Lord LAKE. FUTEH SINGH ALOOWALA was accordingly left to make arrangements with the chiefs of the west, and RUNJEET hastening back in person to Umritsur, met there the fugitive Muhratta, with whom he had no easy part to play. JUSWUNT RAO threatened to continue his flight westward towards the Kabool dominions. Lord LAKE however had arrived on the Beah or Beas, and was prepared to follow, and it was neither convenient nor wise to permit operations of the kind that must ensue, to be carried on in the Punjab. On the other hand RUNJEET SINGH, though he would have proved an useful auxiliary to either party, was sensible of his inability to offer open resistance. In this state of things the relations he maintained with JUSWUNT RAO HOLKUR were friendly, but not encouraging, and that chief being disappointed in the hope of raising the Sikh nation to a co-operation in hostility with him against the British, yielded to the difficulties by which he was surrounded, and made his terms with Lord LAKE in a treaty concluded on the 24th December 1805. Friendly engagements were further exchanged by the British Commander with RUNJEET SINGH, and the Aloowala Sirdar; and in the course of January 1806 the two armies, which had inspired so much alarm in the Punjab, returned to Hindoostan, leaving the Sikh chiefs to celebrate the Hoolee unembarrassed by their presence, and with joy and rejoicings commensurate to the fears they had entertained. RUNJEET SINGH'S excesses at this festival produced a disease which confined him for four months. Towards the end of the rains, he re-appeared in a new field, and entered on measures which in their sequel had material influence on his future destiny and fortunes.

The Rajas of Puteeala and Naba were at feud on account of some lands, situated between the village of Doluddee and the town and fort of Naba. The Jheend chief, Raja BHAG SINGH, was the ally of Naba, and so were the Ladwa and Kythul chiefs, but their united forces were unequal to a contest with their powerful neighbour of Puteeala. In this extremity, BHAG SINGH, of Jheend, the maternal uncle of RUNJEET, was deputed to invite his assistance to the weaker party; and, the Dusera was no sooner over, than the ruler of Lahôr hastened across the Sutlej to take part in this quarrel. He passed the river at Loodeeana, and mastering the place, presented it to Raja BHAG SINGH in exclusion of Ranee NOOROON-NISSA, mother of RAO ILIAS, to whom it had belonged. Saneewal was next seized from another defenceless widow,* this class of occupants being regarded by RUNJEET as his legitimate prey. The place was given in Jageer to MOHKUM CHUND DEWAN, but restored afterwards on realization of a Nuzurana of 30,000 Rupees. Driving the Puteeala troops out of Doluddee, the invader approached Munsoorpoor, where Maha Raja SAHEB SINGH, successor to UMUR SINGH, was in position with his main body. The Maha Raja, by a sum of money and the present of a piece of artillery, propitiated the Lahôr chief, and JUSWUNT SINGH, of Naba, contributed also to satisfy his cupidity, whereupon he was induced to remove the scourge of his ill organized all-ravaging army back into the Punjab. Doluddee was restored to Puteeala at the intercession of Raja BHAG SINGH, and RUNJEET SINGH taking the opportunity to pass the Dewalee and perform his ablutions in the holy tank of Thanesur, re-crossed the

* MAEE LUCH,HMEE, widow of SODHA SINGH—She invited the aid of RUNJEET SINGH, being at issue with her son, who held her at the time in confinement.

Sutlej after that festival, and bent his course via Rahoon, the residence of TARA SINGH GHYBA* to the holy fires of Juwala Mookhee. Here he met Raja SUNSAR CHUND, of Kangra, who solicited his aid against UMUR SINGH, the Goorkha commander, before whom all the chiefs of the hills, from the Gogra to the Sutlej, had fallen in succession, and whose detachments were then ravaging Kangra. The price demanded by RUNJEET for his services being deemed excessive, the interview led to no present arrangement between the chiefs, but as the difficulties of the Hill Raja increased, the negociation was afterwards renewed.

The year 1807 was marked by the lapse and resumption of Pursroor and Chumara, possessions of NUR SINGH deceased, an old Sikh Sirdar. A Jageer for mere subsistence was assigned to the son. RUNJEET next prepared a formidable expedition against Kasoor, which had long been a thorn in the side of his power, and from the conquest of which, as being a Moosulman possession, he hoped for an access of credit and popularity amongst his own sect and nation. In February 1807 he invaded the territory with a large force, and KOOTUB-OOD-DEEN was compelled to shut himself up in his fortress at Kasoor. Internal seditions and broils completed the ruin of this Puthan family, and in March the chief surrendered at discretion. He was left in possession of a small territory south of the Sutlej, and bound to furnish a contingent of troops on demand. Kasoor itself and

* Captain WADE states that TARA SINGH died during this expedition, and that on this occasion RUNJEET SINGH made an acquisition of eight lakhs of Rupees in cash, and of the jewels of the deceased chief, which were of great value. The treasure is alleged to be the first of any extent that was so obtained. Captain MURRAY, however, places the death of TARA SINGH in 1807-8, during the second expedition of RUNJEET SINGH across the Sutlej, and Captain W. appears to have confounded the two visits.

all the territory held by the family in the Punjab was resumed, and assigned for the present in Jageer to NYAL SINGH Utharawala. From Kasoor, RUNJEET SINGH proceeded S. W. towards Mooltan, and occupied and kept garrisons in various dependencies of that government. In April the town of Mooltan was mastered, but the governor held out the fort, into which the principal inhabitants had retired with their valuables. Being unprovided with the means of siege, RUNJEET accepted a sum of money from MOZUFFUR KHAN, and returned to Lahôr in May. In the interval before the rains, he detached a force against Deena-nugur under the Kangra hills, and levied exactions in that neighbourhood from several Sikh and mountain chiefs, who had hitherto enjoyed immunity from their dependence on the Ghunee Misul, with the head of which, SUDA KOONWUR, RUNJEET stood in such close relation. The measure gave offence to that lady, and the foundation was thus laid for the differences and intrigues which led eventually to her ruin.

The wife of the Puteeala Raja was an ambitious intriguing woman who had long sought to set aside her husband, or at least to procure the assignment of a separate territory for her minor son KURUM SINGH. When JUSWUNT RAO HOLKUR passed through Puteeala on his way to the Punjab, she had endeavoured to make him instrumental to her views, and that wily chief made the state of things which prevailed, conducive to his own enrichment, but being pressed for time, in consequence of the approach of Lord LAKE, he left matters between the Raja and Ranee as they were. The quarrel being now renewed, the Ranee sent, in the rains of 1807, to invite RUNJEET SINGH to espouse her cause, promising him a famous brass piece of ordnance belonging to the family, and which bore the name of KUREE KAHN, and, also a diamond necklace of known value, as the price of his assistance. The Lahôr chief gladly seized the occasion to interfere, and crossed the Sutlej at Hureeke-Putun, where that river is joined by the Beah. In the month of September, on his route towards Puteeala, he seized all the remaining possessions of the deceased ILIAS-RAEE, and distributed them amongst his dependents and allies. Before RUNJEET SINGH reached Puteeala, the Raja and Ranee had come to a reconciliation, the latter having, through the mediation of the Jheend and Thanésur chiefs, obtained for her son a separate Jageer of 50,000 Rupees per annum. The Raja now made some demur to render up the gun and necklace promised by his Ranee, but RUNJEET SINGH appealed to the invitation he had received, and his appeal being backed by the condition of his force, the two articles were given up according to promise, though with evident reluctance; and RUNJEET marched with them in possession to reduce Nurayungurh, which was surrendered, and made over to the Aloowala chief, after an unsuccessful attempt to take it by storm, which was attended with a loss of near 400 killed and wounded.

While engaged before Nurayungurh, the old chief TARA SINGH GHYBA, who was serving with RUNJEET SINGH, died, and his followers secretly conveyed the corpse across the Sutlej to his fort of Rahoon, where the funeral obsequies were performed, and the widow and sons made preparation to maintain their possessions. While the body however was yet on the pyre, RUNJEET SINGH's detachment, which had followed on the event being ascertained, arrived to demand a surrender of treasures, and to enforce a resumption of the chief's territory. After a slight resistance, the family was compelled to submit, and though the sons at first received a small provision for subsistence, they were soon deprived of even this means of support, and have since lived in indigence. On his route back from Nurayungurh, RUNJEET SINGH seized Moonda, south of the Sutlej, from the son of DHURUM SINGH, and sold it to the Jheend Sirdar: and Bhulolpoor and Bhurtgurh were similarly taken from BHUGHAEEL SINGH'S widow. In December, RUNJEET SINGH returned to Lahôr, and was presented by his wife, MEHTAB-KOONWUR, with twins. The boys were named SHEER SINGH and TARA SINGH, but RUNJEET has never fully acknowledged them as his own offspring. MEHTAB-KOONWUR'S fidelity had for some time been suspected by her husband, and she had, in consequence, been living with her mother, SUDA KOONWUR. The report ran, that the boys were procured by the latter from a carpenter and weaver, and were produced as born to her daughter, the public having for some time previously been prepared for the birth, by reports circulated of MEHTAB being with child. SHEER SINGH has latterly been honored with military commands and a Jageer, and was fortunate in having been the leader of the expedition, wherein the Mohummedan pretender, SEYUD AHMED was slain in 1831; but neither before nor since this event, has he ever been recognized by RUNJEET as his own son, and TARA SINGH is treated with uniform neglect.

The commencement of 1808 was marked by the seizure of Pŭthān Kot, under the Kangra hills, belonging to JYMUL GHUNEA, and by exactions from chiefs in the hills and plains in that direction. MOHKUM CHUND DEWAN was employed simultaneously in settling arrangements with the dependents of the Duleeala Misul, at the head of which TARA SINGH GHYBA had continued, while he lived. Most of the feudatories were confirmed on their agreeing to transfer their allegiance, and furnish contingents of horse to be constantly in attendance. Seeal-Kot and Sheikhoopoora, south of the Sutlej, were next seized, and annexed to the immediate territory of the Lahôr chief by MOHKUM CHUND, and the Dewan being kept in the field during the rains, seized various other places on both sides of the Sutlej, from the Anundpoor Mukawal valley downwards, and confirmed to his master all that had formerly belonged to TARA SINGH or to BHUGHAEEL SINGH.

The extensive permanent occupations and usurpations, thus made by RUNJEET SINGH on the east and south banks of the Sutlej, excited the alarm of the Sikh chiefs, situated between that river and the Jumna, and, after a conference, it was determined by them, to send a mission to Dehlee, composed of Raja BHAG SINGH, of Jheend, BHAEE LAL SINGH, of Kythul, and CHYN SINGH DEWAN, of Puteeala, in order to solicit that their possessions might be taken under the protection of the British Government. The mission reached Dehlee, and waited on Mr. SETON, the Resident, in March 1808. The answer they received, though not decisive, was encouraging to their hope, that the Lahôr ruler would not be suffered to extend his usurpations eastward, to their prejudice and eventual annihilation. Intelligence of this mission, however, no sooner reached Lahôr, than RUNJEET SINGH, feeling disquieted, dispatched agents to invite the three chiefs who composed it to wait upon him, that he might endeavour to allay their fears. They accordingly went to his camp at Umritsur, where they were received with marked favor and attentions, and no effort was spared in the endeavour to detach them from the design of forming any connexion with the British Government.

Pending these transactions, the alarm of an invasion of India being meditated by the French Emperor, NAPOLEON BUONAPARTE, becoming rife, Lord MINTO determined to send missions to ascertain the condition of the countries intervening, and the feeling of the rulers, chiefs, and people. The growing power of RUNJEET SINGH, whose authority was now completely established in the Punjab, made it essential to include his court, and the collision threatened by the recent proceedings and known designs of RUNJEET, east of the Sutlej, formed an additional motive for deputing a British Agent to Lahôr. Mr. now Sir CHARLES METCALFE, was the negociator selected on this occasion, and the announcement of the intended deputation was received by RUNJEET SINGH, while the Jheend and Kythul chiefs were in attendance on him. To them the contents of the despatch were communicated, and the matter formed the subject of much anxious conference and deliberation. It was determined to receive Mr. METCALFE at Kasoor, whither RUNJEET marched for the purpose in September 1808. On the envoy's arrival, he was received with the usual attentions, but had scarcely found the opportunity to enter on the subjects proposed for discussion with the Sikh chief, when the latter suddenly broke up his camp from Kasoor, and crossed the Sutlej with his army. Fureed-Kot was immediately occupied by him and made over to SUDA KOONWUR in ejection of GOOLAB SINGH, and RUNJEET then proceeded against the Moosulman possession of Muler Kotila. The Puthan family holding it was reduced to extremity, and agreed to a large money payment, giving a bond of a lakh of rupees, to which the Puteeala Raja was induced, by the deposit of some strongholds, to be security. Mr. METCALFE accompanied RUNJEET SINGH to Fureed-Kot, but refused to countenance any military operations east of the Sutlej. He accordingly remained near that river until his Government should determine what to do in the juncture, and addressed in the interval a strong remonstrance against such aggressions, committed in the very face of his proposition to make the matter the subject of discussion and negociation between the Governments. In the mean time RUNJEET SINGH continued his progress to Umbala, which with its dependencies, he seized, and made over to the Naba and Kythul chiefs. He then exacted tribute from Shahabad and Thanesur, and returning by Puteeala, made a brotherly exchange of turbands with the weak RAJA SAHEB SINGH. After this expedition he again gave Mr. METCALFE the meeting at Umritsur. The Government at Calcutta had in October determined on its course, and the envoy was now instructed to avow, that the country between the Sutlej and the Jumna was under British protection, and although that Government had no design to require the surrender of possessions occupied before its interposition, it must insist on the restoration of all that had been seized during the late expedition of RUNJEET SINGH. To enforce this demand, and support the negociation, a body of troops was advanced to the frontier under Colonel, afterwards Sir DAVID OCHTERLONY, and an army of reserve was formed and placed under the command of Major General ST. LEGER, to be prepared for any extended operations, the activity, and supposed hostile designs of RUNJEET SINGH might render necessary.

Colonel OCHTERLONY crossed the Jumna at Booreea on the 16th January 1809, and as he approached Umbala, RUNJEET SINGH's detachment left there retired to the Sutlej. Taking en route the several places visited by the Sikh army, the British commander reached Loodeeana on the Sutlej, and took up a position there on the 18th February following. His march was hailed by the people and chiefs, as affording the promise of future protection and tranquillity, and they vied with one another in the display of their gratitude and satisfaction.

Up to this period, RUNJEET SINGH had maintained in the conferences to which the envoy was admitted, that the Jumna, and not the Sutlej, was the proper boundary of the British possessions, and that in right of his supremacy over the Sikh nation, no less than as Governor of Labôr, he was warranted in asserting feudal superiority over all the chiefs of that nation between those two rivers. The existing independence of Puteeala and the other principalities, had no weight in argument with a chief, whose domination was the right to plunder and usurp, according to the condition of his army, and who aimed only to secure himself this. The arrival of Colonel OCHTERLONY on the Sutlej, however, opened his eyes to a new fear, which was, that if he longer resisted, offers of protection might be made to chiefs in the Punjab, which would effectually curb his ambitious views, and must involve him in collision—and, perhaps, hostility, with a

I 2

power he never thought himself capable of seriously opposing in the field. His resolutions were hastened by an event that occurred in his camp. The Mohurrum, the first and sacred month of the Mohummedans, commenced in 1809 towards the end of February, and the followers of this faith, in the suite of the envoy, prepared to celebrate the deaths of HUSUN and HOOSEIN, the two sons of ULEE, with the usual ceremonies. The *Akalees*, or fanatic priests of the Sikhs, took umbrage at this performance of Mooslim rites in the Sikh camp, and at Umritsur; and collecting in a body, headed by PHOOLA SINGH, a bigot of notorious turbulence, they opened a fire of matchlocks, and attacked the envoy's camp. The escort was called out, and though composed of two companies of Native Infantry and sixteen troopers only, this small body charged and routed their party, after which, the biers were buried with the usual forms. RUNJEET himself came up at the close of the fight; and immediately it was over, advanced in person to make apologies to the envoy, expressing his admiration of the discipline and order displayed by the British detachment, and promising his best exertions to prevent any repetition of such disorders. The circumstance made an impression on his mind as to the unfitness of his own troops to cope with those under European discipline, and determined him to secure peace and friendship at the sacrifices demanded.

The British Government were sensible, that, having interfered to impose restraints on the ambition of RUNJEET SINGH, it had little to expect from his friendship in case of any necessity arising to arm against invasion from the west. Had danger, indeed, from that quarter been more imminent, it would probably have been deemed politic to extend our direct influence farther into the Punjab, in reduction of the power of a chief who showed himself so unfriendly. But by the time arrangements had to be concluded, the apprehension of any necessity of preparation for such an event had worn off, and the only object that remained was, to secure our own frontier, and for the credit of our power to take redress for the offensive aggressions which the Lahôr ruler had recently committed east of the Sutlej. Runjeet Singh expressed a strong desire at this time to obtain a written pledge of our pacific and friendly intentions towards himself; and the restoration of the places seized during his late inroad having been obtained from him, a short treaty declaratory of mutual peace and friendship was concluded by the envoy, at Umritsur, on the 25th April, 1809. It was to the following effect:—

After the usual preamble expressive of the desire for peace, and stating by whom the engagement was settled,

"Article the First.—Perpetual friendship shall subsist "between the British Government and the State of Lahôr: "the latter shall be considered with respect to the former, to be on the footing of the most favored powers, "and the British Government will have no concern with "the territories and subjects of the Raja to the northward of the river Sutlej.

"Article Second.—The Raja will never maintain in "the territory, which he occupies on the left bank of the "Sutlej, more troops than are necessary for the internal "duties of the territory, nor commit or suffer any encroachment on the possessions or rights of the chiefs in its "vicinity.

" Article Third.—In the event of a violation of any of " the preceding articles, or of a departure from the rules " of friendship on the part of either State, this treaty shall " be considered to be null and void." The fourth and last article, provides for the exchange of ratifications.

The treaty being concluded, Mr. METCALFE came away on the 1st May following. All further discussions with RUNJEET SINGH were then dropped, and it became a principle in all relations with this chief to confine communications, as much as possible, to friendly letters and the exchange of presents, but the British officers on the frontier, were instructed to watch the proceedings of RUNJEET SINGH, and to require instant redress, in case of any infringement of the terms of the treaty, by interference with, or encroachment on the rights and territories of Chiefs and Sirdars, east or south of the river Sutlej. The continued prosecution of this course of policy to the present date, has weaned the chief from all apprehension of danger to his own authority, from the ulterior views for which he long gave us credit; and there is now established between the two powers as complete and perfect a good-fellowship as can exist with states constituted like those of India. It is based however on no better foundation than the personal character of RUNJEET SINGH, and his personal conviction that the British Government desires to see him prosperous and powerful, and would regard the extinction of his rule, and the confusion and convulsions which must follow, as a serious evil of mischievous influence to itself. Of this however, more hereafter.

CHAPTER FIFTH.

A. D. 1809 to 1811.

British arrangements with the Chiefs east of the Sutlej. Transactions in the Punjab tending to the further aggrandizement of Runjeet Singh.

THE declarations with which the British force under Colonel OCHTERLONY advanced to the Sutlej, were in strict conformity with the application, made by the chiefs occupying the country between the Indus and Sutlej, through the mission deputed by them to Dehlee in March 1808. Protection was promised, and no demand of tribute or of contribution of any kind made, to defray the charges incurred by the obligation to afford it. The recency of their experience of the rapacity of a Sikh army, and the conviction that there could be no security to themselves, and still less to their families, under a ruler like the chief who had now the ascendant in the Sikh nation, made all the Sirdars rejoice that their prayer had been acceded to by the British Government; and the advance of its forces to the Sutlej was looked upon in consequence with no jealousy, but as a measure necessary to effect the purpose contemplated.

A treaty having been now concluded with RUNJEET SINGH, it became necessary to fix, somewhat more specifically than had been hitherto done, the relations that were to subsist henceforward between the protecting power and its protected dependents. It was determined to give the desired explanation of the views of the British Government on this subject, by a general proclamation, rather than by entering into any separate engagement with the numerous chiefs affected by the measure. Accordingly on the 6th May 1809, an *Italanama*, or general declaration, was circulated to the Sirdars, intimating to them as follows.

First. That the territories of Sirhind and *Malooa,* (the designation assumed by the Sikhs of Puteeala, Naba, Jheend, and Kythul) had been taken under British protection, and RUNJEET SINGH had bound himself by treaty to exercise in future no interference therein.

Second. That it was not the intention of the British Government to demand any tribute from the Chiefs and Sirdars benefiting by this arrangement.

Third. That the Chiefs and Sirdars would be permitted to exercise, and were for the future secured in, the rights and authorities they possessed in their respective territories prior to, and at the time of the declaration of protection by the British Government.

Fourth. That the Chiefs and Sirdars should be bound to offer every facility and accommodation to British troops and detachments, employed in securing the protection guaranteed, or for purposes otherwise connected with the general interests of the state, whenever the same might be marched into, or stationed in, their respective territories.

Fifth. In case of invasion or war, the Sirdars were to join the British standard with their followers, whenever called upon.

Sixth. Merchants conveying articles, the produce of Europe, for the use of the detachments at Loodeeana, or of any other British force or detachment, should not be subject to transit duty, but must be protected in their passage through the Sikh country.

Seventh. In like manner horses for the cavalry when furnished with passports from competent officers, must be exempt from all tax.

The above declaration being published and circulated, became the charter of rights, to which the chiefs have since looked, and appealed, for the settlement of all questions that have arisen between them and the British Government. The matters specifically provided for, were those that immediately pressed. There has been much however of intricate dispute between rival candidates for Sirdarees ;—between chiefs who had divided their territory before the declaration of protection was published, and had bound themselves to their co-proprietors by mutual obligations ; between chiefs and their dependents of the Sikh nation, as well as Zumeendars, as to the extent of right and authority possessed at the time of the declaration of protection ;—and, perhaps more than all, boundary disputes and quarrels regarding participated rights. These differences, whenever they have arisen, have required adjustment and arbitration by the British officers on the spot, and have formed the subject of continual references to the Supreme Government at Calcutta. The regulation of successions was also a matter, that from the first required to be undertaken by the protecting authority, and failing heirs of any kind according to Sikh custom and law, the escheat is considered to fall to the protecting state.

Until the year 1812, the duties of protection, and the settlement of these mutual disputes, though giving constant employment to Colonel OCHTERLONY, the British officer, appointed superintendent of Sikh affairs, produced nothing of sufficient moment to require relation. In that year, however, the disorders in Puteeala consequent upon the Raja's imbecility, produced a crisis that called for an exertion of authoritative interference. The protected territory was invaded by a public depredator, for whose punishment and expulsion the Puteeala Raja was called upon to furnish a quota of horse. This chief holds territory yielding a revenue of more than thirty lakhs of rupees, yet the whole force he could furnish on the occasion consisted only of two hundred horse of the very worst description, and these arrived so late in the field as to be of no use. Colonel OCHTERLONY, taking with him the Chiefs of Jheend and Naba, proceeded to Puteeala to remonstrate with Muha Raja SAHEB SINGH upon the evidence of inefficiency afforded by this state of things, and it was endeavoured to persuade him to discard the low favorites who ate up his revenues, and prevented those better disposed from carrying on any consistent system of government, and from introducing the desired improvements into the administration. The attempt to procure a change of ministers by persuasion failed, but the Raja made many professions of a determination to exert himself to effect the desired reforms. Being left again to himself, his conduct became so violent and irregular, as to betray symptoms of an aberration of reason, and the Colonel was compelled to proceed again to his capital, in order to allow his outraged subjects and dependents to put things on a better footing, and to prevent the Raja's removal from power from producing convulsions, or a breach of the general tranquillity. SAHEB SINGH was now deposed, and placed under limited restraint. ASKOOR RANEE, his wife, in association with a shrewd Brahmin minister named NUNDEE RAO, was appointed regent for the heir-apparent, the present Raja, KURUM SINGH, who was then a minor, and affairs were conducted in his name. Maharaja SAHEB SINGH died a few months after his deposal. The Ranee's doubtful reputation for chastity, and known character for turbulence and intrigue, made her administration unpopular, while the profusions of SAHEB SINGH had secured him many partisans. Hence the part taken by the British Superintendent in the establishment of this scheme of administration, although his motives were appreciated by the discerning, made a great sensation amongst the Sikhs, by the lower order of whom, and particularly by the turbulent, and designing, the Raja's removal from power was regarded as an act of tyranny and injustice, produced by intrigue, and influenced by worse motives. When Colonel OCHTERLONY was at Puteeala, in prosecution of these measures, he was attacked in his palanquin by an Akâlee fanatic, who with his drawn sword had nearly taken the Colonel's life. He escaped, however, with slight wounds by seizing hold of the sword, and the assassin being secured, was sentenced to be confined for life at Dehlee.

In the above notice of occurrences east of the Sutlej, the events of the Punjab have been anticipated. It is now time to resume the narrative of RUNJEET SINGH'S usurpations, and of the expeditions and enterprizes by which he consolidated and extended his dominions.

The first operation in which the Lahôr army was engaged after Mr. METCALFE'S departure in May, 1809, was against Kangra, in the hills; but before moving in that direction, RUNJEET SINGH gave order to place the fort of [illegible]lôr, on the Sutlej opposite to Loodeeana, and also Govind-gurh, in Umritsur, where his treasure was, and still is deposited, in the best possible condition for defence. The walls were rebuilt, and a deep ditch, scarped with masonry, was added to the works of both strongholds, which being completed, the chief moved into the hills.

Kangra was at this time besieged by UMUR SINGH THÂPA, the Goorkha commander, but held out against him. The garrison, however, being reduced to extremity, Raja SUNSAR CHUND tendered the place to RUNJEET SINGH, on condition of his lending troops to raise the siege, and expel the Goorkhas from the territory west and north of the Sutlej. The engagement was gladly entered into by RUNJEET, and on the 28th May, he arrived with his army at Puthan-Kot, in the Jalundhur Turaee, a possession of JYMUL GHUNEEA, which he seized and confiscated. Thence he sent a detachment to strengthen the forces of the confederate hill chiefs, who were at the time engaged in the attempt to cut off UMUR SINGH'S supplies, and so compel his retirement. UMUR SINGH made an effort to deprecate this interference, and sent to offer to RUNJEET SINGH, a money equivalent for Kangra. The fort, however, had a value in the eye of the aspiring Sikh, which made him regardless of the temptation offered to his avarice. This stronghold has the reputation in Hindoostan of being impregnable. SUNSAR CHUND, notwithstanding his engagement, could not reconcile it to his honor to part with the fort, and evaded RUNJEET SINGH'S importunity for a Sikh garrison to be admitted within its walls. In August, having proceeded in person to the vicinity, and being still put off with excuses, the Sikh's patience became exhausted. He accordingly placed the Raja's son, who was in attendance with him, under restraint, and having ascertained that the army of UMUR SINGH was in great straight for supplies, and short of ammunition, he directed a chosen body of Sikhs to advance boldly to the gate, and demand entrance. They suffered considerably in killed and wounded as they ascended, but on reaching the gate were received into the fort, which thus fell into the power of RUNJEET SINGH, on the 24th of August 1809. UMUR SINGH being foiled in his purpose, and having no desire to involve himself with the Sikhs, came to an understanding with RUNJEET SINGH, and, having secured by his connivance the means of transport, retired across the Sutlej.

On the 31st of September, RUNJEET SINGH having completed arrangements with the hill chiefs, and taken the necessary steps to secure his possession of Kangra, returned to the Jalundhur Dooab, and seized the Jageer of BHUGHAEEL SINGH'S eldest widow, who had recently died there: his Dewan was similarly employed, in seizing the districts of BHOOP SINGH Fyzoollapoorea, whose person he secured treacherously at an interview.

It was at this time, and influenced apparently by observation of the efficiency and discipline maintained by the British Sipahees with Mr. METCALFE, that RUNJEET SINGH commenced the formation of regular battalions on the British model, entertaining for the purpose *Poorbees*, that is, natives of the Gangetic provinces, and Sikhs from the other side of the Sutlej. These he formed into bodies of three and four hundred, and procured deserters from the British ranks, whom he employed to drill them, and nominated to be commanders with superior pay. His artillery was also formed into a separate corps under a Darogha, or superintendent; and the cavalry attached to himself, he divided into two classes, one called the Ghor-chur Suwars, and the other the Ghor-chur-Khas, the first being paid in money, and the latter by Jageers, both classes however were mounted on horses, the property of the state.

JODH SINGH, of Vuzeerabad, died towards the close of 1809; and on the first day of the new year RUNJEET SINGH arrived there to enforce the resumption of his territorial possessions. A large sum of money was tendered by GUNDHA SINGH, the son of the deceased, as the price of his confirmation, and the Lahôr chief's avarice being tempted, he refrained from present occupation of the estates, and conferred the Shâl and Turband of investiture on the heir. A dispute between the father and son of Goojrat affording the opportunity, he succeeded in expelling both, and in confiscating that territory; after which, he proceeded to the country east of the Jihlum, as far as Saheewal, and exacted tribute and contributions from the Balooch and other Moosulman chiefs of that quarter.

On the 2nd of February, in the midst of these operations, it was announced to RUNJEET SINGH, that SHAH-SHOOJA was approaching to seek refuge in his territory, having been compelled to yield to the ascendancy acquired by his brother, SHAH MAHMOOD, through the vigour and talents of the Vuzeer FUTEH KHAN. The Ex-Shah joined the camp of RUNJEET at Khooshab on the day following, viz. the 3rd February 1810, and was received with much outward respect, RUNJEET having gone forth in person to conduct him in, and sending a Zeeafut of 1250 Rs. to his tents upon his alighting. The Shah, however, returned to Rawul Pindee on the 12th February, to join his brother ZUMAN SHAH, leaving RUNJEET SINGH to prosecute his operations against the Moosulman chiefs east of the Indus. A succour of men and money had been tendered by the Government of Kashmeer, and by ATA MOHUMMUD KHAN, son of the old Vuzeer SHEER MOHUMMUD; and, thus aided, SHAH SHOOJA made an attack on Peshawur, and was received there on the 20th of March. In September following, however, he was expelled by MOHUMMUD UZEEM, brother of FUTEH KHAN, and driven again across the Indus, whereupon he endeavoured to obtain admission into Mooltan without effect. In the mean time, however, events of interest had occurred in the Punjab.

The Saheewal chief had accepted terms from RUNJEET SINGH on the 25th of January, but failing to pay the entire amount agreed upon (80,000 rupees,) that town was invested on the 7th February. FUTEH KHAN, the Sirdar, surrendered; but upon some demur in giving up a dependency of Saheewal, named Lukhomut, he was sent in irons to Lahôr, and kept there in close confinement with all his family, the whole of his estate being sequestered. On the 15th February, RUNJEET'S army was before Ooch,h, the proprietors of which place, Seyuds of Geelan and Bokhara, waited on the Sikh with horses, and this conduct, added to the estimation in which their tribe is held for sanctity by both Hindoos and Mohummedans, propitiated the chief, and they were left in possession under an engagement to pay tribute. On the 20th February, such was the rapidity with which RUNJEET SINGH prosecuted his measures, the whole Sikh army was before Mooltan ravaging the surrounding territory, consequently upon a refusal by MOZUFFUR KHAN to pay the sum of three lakhs of rupees, which had been demanded from him: RUNJEET SINGH now demanded the fort of Mooltan, declaring that he desired it for SHAH SHOOJA, to whom MOZUFFUR KHAN was bound, and had engaged to render it. This specious pretext made no change in MOZUFFUR KHAN'S resolution to defend the place to the utmost. RUNJEET SINGH reconnoitred, and marked out ground for different batteries, and lines of approach, assigning them to different chiefs, with the promise of rich Jageers to those who made the quickest advance, and most impression. Arrangements were made to secure the transmission of supplies by water, as well as by land, from Lahôr and Umritsur, and every thing betokened a determination in the Sikh chief to master this important possession. The garrison was not disheartened, but made the best dispositions possible for defence. A large supply of grain had been laid in, and the fort contained an abundance of fresh water. The little impression made on the walls by the Sikh artillery confirmed the courage of the defenders. The great Bhungee gun, which discharged a ball of two and a half maunds *kuchha*, had been brought down for the siege, but the materials for such an operation were so defective in the Sikh army, and the necessary science and experience were so wanting, that RUNJEET SINGH having suffered the loss of many valuable men and officers, and particularly of ATAR SINGH, a favorite and confidential companion, who was blown up in a mine, was compelled to grant terms to MOZUFFUR KHĀN, and retired on receiving payment of a lakh and 80,000 rupees. On the 25th of April, he returned to Lahôr, mortified greatly by his ill success, and throwing the blame on his officers and Jageerdars. He now devoted himself to increase the number of his regular battalions, and formed a corps of Sikhs, called, "*Orderly Khas,*" or select orderlies, to whom he gave superior pay, and the advantage of carrying his *dustuks*, or orders, to chiefs, and districts, on whom they were thus billeted at high rates. A horse artillery was likewise formed, and improvements were set on foot in every branch of the service, which were all closely superintended by RUNJEET in person.

GUNDHA SINGH, who in January preceding, had secured by the sacrifice of his father's treasures, a temporary confirmation of his estates, did not long enjoy what he purchased so dearly. In June 1810, a strong detachment was sent to Vuzeerabad, and the entire possessions of the late JODH SINGH were sequestered, a few villages only being left to afford subsistence to the youthful victim of this insidious policy. The surviving widow of BHUGAEEL SINGH, Ranee RAM-KOONWUR, was at the same time expelled from Buhadurpoor, which she held as a Jageer for subsistence. She took refuge at Loodeeana, and obtained a few villages which had belonged to her husband, on the protected side of the Sutlej.

After the Dussera, in the month of October following, RUNJEET SINGH moved in person to Ramnugur, on the Chunab. and summoned to his presence NIDHAN SINGH of Huttoo. The Chief refused attendance, except under guarantee of a Sodee, or Sikh priest, whereupon his fort of Duskut was invested on the 17th October. RUNJEET SINGH'S batteries, however, opened against the place without avail in producing a surrender, and an attempt made to influence the garrison, by severities, and ill usage of their wives and families, who fell into the besieger's power, was equally ineffective. The Sikh Priest BYDEE JUMEEYUT SINGH was then employed to mediate for the submission of this spirited Chief, and upon his guarantee and the promise of a Jageer, the Sirdar waited on RUNJEET SINGH, who regardless of the solemnity of the engagement he had contracted, put him in irons on the 30th October. In the beginning of November, BAGH SINGH Huloowala, with his son SOOBHA SINGH, who were in camp with their followers, fell under the displeasure of the Lahôr Chief, and were placed under restraint, and all their territorial possessions confiscated; after which RUNJEET SINGH returned to his capital, and detached MOHKUM-CHUND Dewan to enforce the collection of tribute, and to complete arrangements in the hills, where the Rajas of Bhimbhur and Rajaoree, and the tribe of Chibh-Bhào, were refractory.

In December 1810, SAHEB SINGH, who had been expelled from Goojrat, was invited to return, and invested with a considerable Jageer, and BAGH SINGH Huloowala was released from confinement, and similarly honored. In the same month, the release of NIDHAN SINGH was obtained by the Bydee priests, who felt their honor concerned in his treatment, after one of their body had been inveigled to give a personal guarantee. They accordingly sat Dhurna on RUNJEET, until he consented to release his prisoner: NIDHAN SINGH would, however, accept no Jageer, or stipend, but retired from the Lahôr dominions, and took service with the governor of Kashmeer.

In January 1811, FUTEH KHAN, of Saheewal, was liberated with his family at the intercession of an Oodasee priest, and retired to Buhawulpoor. A small Jageer was likewise conferred on DHURUM SINGH, the ejected proprietor of Dhurum-Kot, in the Jalundhur, after which, RUNJEET SINGH proceeded on a tour to Pind-Dadur-Khan, in which vicinity he captured three small forts belonging to Moosulman Chiefs ; but on the 24th February, intelligence reached his camp, that SHAH MUHMOOD had crossed the Indus with 12,000 Afghans, before whom the inhabitants of the country were flying. RUNJEET SINGH immediately took up a position at Rawul-Pindee, and deputed his secretary, HUKEEM UZEEZ-OOD-DEEN, to enquire of the Shah his views in this incursion. This agent was crossed by emissaries from the Shah, on their way to Rawul-Pindee, for the purpose of explaining, that the punishment of ATA MOHUMMUD, and the governors of Atuk and Kashmeer, who had aided SHAH SHOOJAH'S late attempt on Peshawur, was the only object of the present march; whereupon RUNJEET SINGH, being relieved from his apprehensions, waited upon the Shah, and after a friendly interview, both returned to their respective capitals. RUNJEET SINGH found at Lahôr, a carriage from Calcutta, which had been forwarded as a present from the Governor General, Lord MINTO. This being the first vehicle on springs, in which he had ever sat, the novelty and ease of motion were highly gratifying to him, and an agent was deputed to Calcutta to make suitable acknowledgments for the present. The Chief, however, was too wily to adopt generally this mode of conveyance, which would have imposed the necessity of first making roads.

In April and May, RUNJEET SINGH had armies in three directions, one about Kangra, collecting tributes, a second acting against Bhimbhur and Rajaoree, and the third, under his son KHURUK SINGH, accompanied by Dewan MOHKUM CHUND, resuming the possessions of the Nukee Chiefs. RUNJEET SINGH remained in person at his capital, directing the whole, and this period of his life is marked by the sudden rise to favor of a young Gour Brahmin, named KHOOSHHAL SINGH, upon whom the most extravagant gifts were daily lavished, and who was raised to the important and lucrative office of Deohree Wala, or Lord Chamberlain, with the rank of Raja, and vested besides with extensive Jageers. RUNJEET SINGH had ever led a most dissolute life; his debaucheries, particularly during the Hoolee and Dussera, were shameless, and the scenes exhibited on such occasions openly before the Court, and even in the streets of Lahôr, were the conversation of Hindoostan, and rival the worst that is reported in history of the profligacies of ancient Rome. The Chief himself would parade the streets in a state of inebriety, on the same elephant with his courtezans, amongst whom one named MORA acquired most celebrity by her shamelessness, and by the favor with which she was treated. Coin was at one time struck in her name, and her influence seemed without bounds. In August of this year, however, she was discarded, and sent to be incarcerated in Puthan-Kot, and the favor she enjoyed seemed to be transferred to the Brahmin youth and his brothers. If this conduct in the ruler of Lahôr should excite surmises, as to the motives of the extraordinary attachment shown to a graceful youth of the appearance of KHOOSHHAL SINGH, the reader must yet make allowances for the habits in which the Chief was brought up, and the examples by which he was surrounded. The Sikhs are notoriously addicted to pæderasty, and other unnatural lusts, and the worst that is said of Roman and Grecian indulgence in such propensities, would find a parallel at the Durbars of the Chiefs of this nation on either side of the Sutlej. The truth of history forbids the veil being thrown altogether over such facts and traits of character, howsoever revolting it may be to allude to them. But the reputation of RUNJEET SINGH, though justly, it is feared, tainted with the foul blemish, does not suffer in the eyes of his nation from this cause, howsoever the circumstance may be regarded by strangers.

Of the twelve original Misuls, or confederacies of the Sikhs, there were now remaining in the Punjab, only that of RUNJEET SINGH himself, the Sookurchukea, with the Ghuneea, Ramgurhea, and Aloowala, all closely associated with him, and ranged it may be said under his standard. The Phoolkea and Nihung Misuls, which being settled east of the Sutlej, enjoyed the advantage of British protection, and the Fyzoolla-poorea, which had possessions on both sides that river, and the head of which BOODH SINGH Sirdar had uniformly declined to give his personal attendance on RUNJEET, complete the list which RUNJEET SINGH was aiming further to reduce. The conduct of BOODH SINGH at last brought down upon him the vengeance of the Lahôr ruler. On the 19th September 1811, DEWAN MOHKUM CHUND, attended by JODH SINGH RAM-GURHEEA, and other Sirdars, entered the Jalundhur Dooab, with the declared design of seizing the Fyzoolla-poorea possessions in the Punjab. BOODH SINGH waited not for the attack, but fled immediately to Loodeeana for personal security. His troops, influenced by the point of honor, made a resistance of some days, before surrendering the principal forts of Jalundhur and Puttee, but gave both up on the 6th and 7th of October, before any impression had been made on the walls, or defences, and after a needless sacrifice of lives. BOODH SINGH has since been content with the lot of a protected Sikh chief, living on the means afforded by his possessions East and South of the Sutlej. In December of the same year, NIDHAN SINGH, son of the old Ghuneea Chief JY SINGH, was deprived of the separate Jageer assigned to him, in order to secure the Sirdaree to his elder brother's widow, SUDA KOONWUR. His person was seized and placed under restraint at Lahôr, while a detachment marched to capture his two forts of Hajeepoor and Phoolwara, no tie of affinity being recognized as a motive for deviating from the systematic prosecution of the course of policy, by which it appears

RUNJEET SINGH regulated his conduct, viz. the determination to level into subjects and dependents, owing all to himself, every one who was in a position to assert independence, or who prided himself on a separate origin, and enjoyed patrimonies, won by his own or his ancestor's swords. RUNJEET SINGH, who was himself free spoken, and allowed great latitude in conversation to his courtiers, received at this period a rebuke for the grasping disposition he displayed in his treatment of the old Sikh, Sirdars from JODH SINGH Ramghureea, himself a reduced chief of the class. When taking his leave to join MOHKUM CHUND in the operations against the Fyzoollapooreea Sirdar, RUNJEET SINGH ordered him presents as a mark of favor. He begged, however, with characteristic frankness, that such honors might be dispensed with in his case, for he should deem himself fortunate in these times, if allowed to keep his own turband on his head. RUNJEET SINGH took no offence at this freedom, but smiled and told him to be faithful and of good cheer.

The year 1811 closed with a visit to Lahôr by SHAH ZUMAN, the brother in exile and misfortune of SHAH SHOOJA, with the addition of deprivation of sight. He came with his family and dependents in the course of November, but experiencing only neglect from the Sikh chief, returned soon after to Rawul-Pindee, where he had been residing for some months. SHAH SHOOJA, since his failure in September to obtain entrance or reception at Mooltan, embarked in a desperate attempt to push his fortune again beyond the Indus. He was, however, defeated with the loss of his principal officer, UKRUM KHAN, and was compelled to seek personal safety in secret flight. The brothers had, in the early part of the year, deputed a son of ZUMAN SHAH to Loodeeana, to learn if there was any hope of assistance in men or money from the British Government. The Prince, however, though received with much attention and civility, was distinctly informed, that no such expectations must be entertained by either member of the royal family of Kabool.

CHAPTER SIXTH.

A. D. 1812—1813.

Marriage of Khuruk Singh, the heir-apparent of Runjeet Singh, attended by Colonel Ochterlony. Acquisition of the Kohi-noor Diamond from Shah Shooja. Severe treatment and flight of that Prince to Loodeeana. Conquest of Kashmeer, by Futeh Khan Vuzeer, and acquisition of Attuk, by Runjeet Singh.

In the beginning of the year 1812, the Court of Lahôr was occupied in preparations, for celebrating with due magnificence the marriage of the heir-apparent Koonwur Khuruk Singh, with the daughter of Jymul Ghuneea, the same chief from whom Runjeet Singh had taken Puthan-Kot, in the Jalundhur Turaee. An invitation was sent to Colonel Ochterlony at Loodeeana to honor the ceremonies with his presence, and an envoy being despatched to conduct him to Lahôr, the Colonel crossed the Sutlej on the 23d of January, with a small escort, to which, by particular desire of Runjeet, a galloper gun was attached, the Sikh Chief having intense curiosity to see how this branch of artillery was equipped in the British service. Colonel OCHTERLONY was accompanied by the Rajas of Naba, Jheend, and Kythul, and on arriving near Umritsur on the 28th, received the *Istuqbal*, or meeting of honor, from the Chief of the Sikhs, who had gathered to his court, on this occasion, all his Sirdars, and indeed the whole nation of Sikhs appeared to be assembled to do honor to the nuptials.

The ceremony was performed at the residence of Sirdar JYMUL SINGH in Futehgurh, and, after its conclusion on the 6th of February, the whole party returned to Umritsur. SUDA KOONWUR alone was not present; indisposition was assigned as the reason of her non-attendance on the occasion, but her dissatisfaction at the failure of an attempt to procure from RUNJEET SINGH, her son-in-law, the public acknowledgment during these ceremonies, of the two boys she had brought up as twins born to her daughter, was generally believed to be the true cause of her absence.

RUNJEET SINGH received Colonel OCHTERLONY with marked distinction, appointed his principal officers to show him every object worth seeing at Lahôr, and pressed upon him an invitation to stay and see the festivities of the Hoolee, which would be celebrated in March. The Colonel declined this honor for himself, but the Sikh Chiefs who had come with him gladly accepted it, and the Bhye of Kythul obtained by cunning and intrigue during the orgies, a grant from the Lahôr Ruler of Goojurawul, on the protected side of the Sutlej. The frank confidence displayed by RUNJEET SINGH in his present reception of Colonel OCHTERLONY was much in contrast with the suspicious mistrust with which Mr. METCALFE had been treated. RUNJEET showed the Colonel his troops, and particularly the new battalions he was raising, and further took him over the fortifications of Lahôr, and inspected with him some new works he was constructing for their improvement, and to connect the Juma Musjid with the palace. His prudent Dewan, MOHKUM CHUND, and the Sirdar GUNDHA SINGH, are reported to have remonstrated against the communication of such knowledge, to a professional person of a nation, that might have designs which would enable him to turn it to account adversely. RUNJEET, however, observed with shrewdness, that if such were their sentiments, they should have advised his withholding the invitation altogether from the Colonel, for it was too late to begin now to show distrust.

After the conclusion of these ceremonies and festivities, the armies of Lahôr resumed active operations. KOONWUR KHURUK SINGH was sent with a strong force against Bhimbur and Rajaoree, where SOOLTAN KHAN, the Moosulman holder of the former territory, proved a formidable enemy, having recently overpowered and slain his relation ISMAEEL KHAN, who had been left, as the result of previous operations, in the possession and management of a large portion of the territory. DUL SINCH was at the same time sent with another force to plunder and levy tribute from MUZUFFUR KHAN at Mooltan; and a third under DESA SINGH was again detached to Kangra. RUNJEET SINGH in person made a tour into the Jalundhur Dooab towards the Turaee, whither he summoned various hill chiefs, and made with them fresh arrangements attended with increase of tribute. The resumption of Shoojanpoor from BOODH SINGH BHUGUT was the only operation of that kind effected on this occasion. Returning to Lahôr on the 23d of May, RUNJEET SINGH received intelligence there of the success of KHURUK SINGH against Bhimbur, Jummoo and Ukhnoor. The Koonwur was honored with a grant of these places in Jageer, and he placed them in the management of BHYE RAM SINGH. DUL SINGH had also succeeded in extorting a considerable sum from MOZUFFUR KHAN of Mooltan.

In August of the same year, JYMUL SINGH, the father-in-law of KHURUK SINGH, died suddenly, and it was generally believed, that his death was occasioned by poison administered by his wife. RUNJEET SINGH constituted himself the heir to all the treasure, accumulated by this chief during a long life of parsimony and usurious dealing. Much of his wealth was, at the time of his decease, out at interest with Muhajuns of Umritsur, all of whom were called upon to account with the Lahôr treasury. In the following month the families of the two ex-Shahs of Kabool, i. e. of SHAH ZUMAN and of SHAH SHOOJA sought an asylum at Lahôr. The latter chief had added largely to his experience of adversity. After escaping from the unfortunate enterprize, he had undertaken in September preceding, his person was seized by JUHAN DAD KHAN, the Governor of Attuk, by whom he was sent to his brother ATA MOHUMMUD of Kashmeer, who held him a close prisoner. The helpless SHAH ZUMAN brought both families to the Sikh capital, where RUNJEET SINGH professed much interest in the misfortunes and fate of SHAH SHOOJA, and seemed as if disposed to make an effort against Kashmeer to procure his liberation, and to obtain that province for him. He was then preparing an expedition against Bhimbur, in the Peer-Punjal range of mountains, and the wife of SHAH SHOOJA was led by these professions to believe, and to represent to her husband, that he would find a friend in the ruler of Lahôr. The Shah made his escape from confinement during the operations subsequently undertaken against the valley by FUTEH KHAN Vuzeer, and was led by these hopes to direct his flight towards Lahôr. He made good his way out of Kashmeer, by seeking the Peer-Punjal mountains; where, finding an opportunity to join the force under MOHKUM CHUND, he came down with him to Lahôr, there to experience only new persecutions, excited by the desire kindled in the breast of RUNJEET, to obtain possession of the famous diamond the *Koh-i-Noor*, and other rich jewels ascertained to be still in this Prince's possession. The relation, however, of the means by which these were extorted, belongs to a later period.

After the Dussera, at the close of the rains, the Sikh army was assembled, and led entire by RUNJEET SINGH in person, against the Moosulman Chiefs of Bhimbur and Rajaoree, who, though pressed by the expeditions before directed against them, made head again, immediately the force was withdrawn, and were now assisted by a confederacy of Chiefs and Jageerdars of their faith, and by succour from the Governor of Kashmeer. The possessions of these Chiefs commanded the approaches to the Peer-Punjal mountains, and there is reason to believe that RUNJEET SINGH had even at this time, an eye to the conquest eventually of the valley of Kashmeer, to which the occupation of both Bhimbur and Rajaoree was a necessary preliminary. The Sikh army defeated the confederated Chiefs with great loss, and RUNJEET SINGH pushing his success, occupied both Bhimbur and Rajaoree, in the early part of November, and received the submission of the discomfited Mohummedan Chiefs of both places on the 13th of the month. The rest of the confederates were compelled to fly into Kashmeer, where they were received by the Governor, ATA MOHUMMUD.

FUTEH KHAN, the Vuzeer of SHAH MUHMOOD, was at this time upon the Indus, whither he had come to punish the two brothers, who held Attuk and Kashmeer, for the assistance they had rendered to SHAH SHOOJA, and to recover the two provinces for Kabool. He had sent forward a detachment of 8000 Afghans to Rohtas, and was already planning operations against ATA MOHUMMUD of Kashmeer, when RUNJEET obtained his successes against the Bhimbur and Rajaoree chiefs. It became essential, that engaged as the Lahôr and Kabool forces were so closely upon the same field, the two leaders should come to a mutual explanation of their views and intentions; accordingly RUNJEET SINGH sent agents with an overture for this purpose, and invited the Vuzeer to an interview upon the Jhilum, in order that they might concert a joint expedition against Kashmeer. FUTEH KHAN being no less desirous to come to an understanding with the Sikh, the meeting was agreed upon, and took place on the 1st December, when it was settled that RUNJEET SINGH should place a force, under his Dewan MOHKUM CHUND, at the Vuzeer's disposal in the expedition he meditated, and should give every facility for the passage into Kashmeer, by the passes of Rajaoree, which he had recently subdued. The aid of a detachment of Afghans to be employed afterwards against Mooltan, and a share of the plunder of Kashmeer, were the returns stipulated for this succour. RUNJEET SINGH desired a portion of the revenues of the valley, but the politic Vuzeer objected to any participation in the permanent resources of the province, and preferred agreeing to a Nuzurana of nine lakhs from the spoil expected. Having on these terms secured the assistance of 12,000 Sikhs, under the Dewan MOHKUM CHUND, the Vuzeer proceeded on his expedition, and the joint armies commenced their march, while RUNJEET returned to Lahôr. A heavy fall of snow impeded their progress, and the Sikhs being less inured to the severities of a mountain winter than the northern troops, were outstripped by the Vuzeer; who, penetrating into the valley in February, drove ATA MOHUMMUD from his stockades, and in a short time reduced him to submission, and obtained all the strongholds in the province, without receiving much assistance from MOHKUM CHUND and the Sikhs. RUNJEET SINGH made great rejoicings at Lahôr on receiving news of this success, treating the operation as a joint one, tending equally to his own as to the Vuzeer's glory. A deep intrigue was, however, in progress, which the issue of the Kashmeer expedition brought immediately to light. JUHAN DAD KHAN, the governor of Attuk, despairing after his brother's defeat in Kashmeer, of his own ability to resist the Vuzeer single handed, and knowing he had little favor to expect from him, had previously placed himself in correspondence with RUNJEET SINGH, to whom he promised the fort of Attuk for a Jageer, in case he should be reduced to extremity. RUNJEET, accordingly, when he returned himself to Lahôr, left a detachment under DYA SINGH, in the vicinity of the Indus, to be ready to occupy that important fortress, whenever it should be given up. In March, 1813, RUNJEET SINGH heard that his officer had been admitted, and that the place was held and administered in his name. He accordingly lost no time in reinforcing the detachment, with a strong convoy, containing every thing necessary to place the fort in a complete state of defence, and DEVEE DAS and HUKEEM UZEEZ-OOD-DEEN were sent as commissioners to settle the country surrounding, which formed the dependency of Attuk. FUTEH KHAN Vuzeer cried out against this usurpation, and deeming himself absolved by it, from the conditions upon which he had obtained the co-operation of the Sikhs under the Dewan, he dismissed them without any share of the booty obtained; and then nominating his brother, UZEEM KHAN, governor in Kashmeer, he marched to Attuk, and made upon RUNJEET a demand for its surrender. This was spun out into a negociation—and, of course, evaded by the Sikh. With the Dewan MOHKUM CHUND, SHAH SHOOJA came to Lahôr, where a demand was immediately made upon him, and upon his principal wife, to surrender the Koh-i-noor diamond, a Jageer being promised with a fort as the condition of compliance. The Shah denied that he had it, and the VUFA BEGUM declared, it had been placed in pawn with a Muhajun to obtain supplies for the Shah in his distresses. RUNJEET SINGH disbelieving these assertions, placed guards round the Shah's residence, and allowed no access or egress without strict search. The exiled family, however, being proof against the severity of mere restraint, the prohibition of food was added, and for two days the Shah, with his wives, family, and servants, suffered absolute deprivation; but their firmness was even proof against this trial, and RUNJEET SINGH, from a regard to his own reputation determined to proceed with more art, and ordered food to be supplied. On the first of April, there were produced in his durbar two notes, purporting to be from the Shah to FUTEH KHAN Vuzeer, and to other Afghan chiefs, descriptive of his sufferings, and praying for their efforts for his deliverance. These were stated to have been intercepted, but were generally believed to have been fabricated. It was now assumed to be indispensable to take precautions against the intrigues and machinations of the Shah, and a guard of two companies of Sikhs, from the newly raised corps, being added to that previously set over the premises where he resided, threats of a transfer of the Shah's person to Govind-gurh, with treatment of the most galling and injurious kind were resorted to, in order to enforce compliance with the demand for the jewel. Having tried remonstrance in vain, the Shah next resorted to artifice, and solicited two months' delay, to enable him to procure the diamond from certain Muhajuns with whom it was asserted to be pledged, and he said that some lakhs of rupees must be expended to effect this. RUNJEET SINGH reluctantly consented to allow the time solicited, and severities were accordingly suspended for a season. They were renewed, however, before the period expired, and SHAH SHOOJA, wearied out by them, and seeing that the rapacity of the Sikh would not hesitate even at the sacrifice of his life for its gratification, agreed at last to give up the precious jewel.* Accordingly, on the 1st of June, RUNJEET

* This diamond was one of those described by TAVERNIER, as adorning the Peacock throne at Dehlee. It is the largest known to exist, and is by Hindoos supposed to have belonged to the Pandoos of Mythological celebrity, before it fell into the hands of the Moghul Sovereigns. It is

waited on the Shah, with a few attendants to receive it. He was received by the exiled Prince with much dignity, and both being seated, a pause and solemn silence ensued, which continued for nearly an hour. RUNJEET then getting impatient, whispered to one of his attendants to remind the Shah of the object of his coming. No answer was returned, but the Shah with his eyes made the signal to an Eunuch, who retired, and brought in a small roll, which he set down on the carpet at equal distance between the Chiefs. RUNJEET desired BHOOANEE DAS to unfold the roll, when the diamond was exhibited, and recognized, and the Sikh immediately retired with his prize in hand. The Shah was now left more at liberty, his guard being withdrawn: a letter was, however, intercepted a few days after from Kazee SHEER MOHUMMUD, one of his followers, to MOHUMMUD UZEEM KHAN, the new governor of Kashmeer, containing a proposition to assassinate RUNJEET SINGH, and advising the Vuzeer FUTEH KHAN to make a simultaneous attack on Lahôr. The Sikh sent for one of the Princes of the exiled family, and through him transmitted the letter, with its writer, who had been seized, to the Shah. The Ex-king sent both back, begging of RUNJEET SINGH to punish the Kazee as he might deem fitting. In the idea, that a confession of the Shah's privity would be extorted, the guard on duty were desired to lay on with their shoes and with sticks. The Kazee fainted under the blows he received, declaring, however, to the last, his master's entire innocence, he was then committed to prison, whence

nearly an inch and a half in length, and an inch wide, and rises half an inch from its gold setting. NADIR SHAH robbed the Dehlee family of it, and AHMED SHAH Abdalee got possession of it in the pillage of NADIR SHAH's tents after his assassination.

SHAH SHOOJA after a time purchased his release by a payment of 20,000 rupees.

FUTEH KHAN Vuzeer after his return from Kashmeer, had sat down before Attuk, and pending the negociation at Lahòr, upon his demand for its surrender, closely blockaded the fort. Dewan MOHKUM CHUND had been sent to the vicinity, to act as occasion might require, and in the beginning of July, intelligence was received from him, that the garrison was reduced to such straight for supplies, that, unless very shortly relieved, they must surrender. RUNJEET SINGH held a council upon this, and it was determined to relieve the fort, even at the risk of the attempt producing hostilities with the Vuzeer. Orders to this effect were accordingly sent immediately to the Dewan, who being encamped at Boorhan, marched at break of day on the 12th July 1813, to execute them. On that day he made a short march to an outpost on a rivulet, held by a piquet of the Vuzeer's army, which retired in the night. The Dewan marched again next morning leisurely along the rivulet, that his men might drink, and be always fresh for action, the weather being extremely hot. At ten in the morning, he came to the Indus, at about five miles from the fort. The Kabool army was here drawn up to oppose his further advance, its van being composed of a body of Moolkea Moosulmans, supported by a body of cavalry under DOST MOHUMMED KHAN. The Dewan took up his ground, forming his cavalry in four divisions, and the only battalion of infantry that had yet come up, in square. The Moolkeas immediately made a resolute charge on the battalion, but were received with so heavy a rolling fire as to be driven back with severe loss. The Dewan ordered up for the support of his battalion, some fresh troops, and artillery under Ghousee Khan, which had come in sight, but his order was not obeyed. Dost Mohummud now attacked with his horse, and the Sikhs were sinking before him, when the Dewan in person on his elephant, carried up two guns, which discharging grape checked the Afghans. By this time it was noon, the heat of the sun had become intense, and a strong hot wind blew the dust into the faces of the Afghans. Under these disadvantages, the Vuzeer did not think proper to carry the troops he had in reserve into action, and those who had been engaged being exhausted, the battle ceased. The Vuzeer retired across the Indus to Peshawur, leaving the Dewan free to relieve the fort, which having effected, Mohkum Chund returned to Lahôr in August, to receive the reward of his service, and to prefer his complaint against the officers, whose disobedience had so nearly proved fatal. They received the punishment, attaching to correspondence with the enemy, which was detected as the motive of their so critically holding back from the action.

In the rains of 1813 nothing particular occurred, but toward the close of that season Runjeet Singh commenced preparation for an expedition into Kashmeer. In October he visited Juwala-Mookhee, and Kangra, and thence marched, viâ Seeal-Kot and Vuzeerabad to the Jyhlum, where he summoned all his Jageerdars, and all the tributary hill chiefs, to be in attendance with their respective quotas. Strict muster was taken of each party as it arrived, and fines were imposed if the number was short, or the equipment in any respect deficient. Great preparation had also been made to bring an effective artillery into the field, and to improve that mounted on camels, and the whole having been reviewed, RUNJEET SINGH, on the 11th November, crossed the Jyhlum, and entered the town of Rohtas. The Vuzeer FUTEH KHAN was brought from Peshawur by these preparations to the Derajat, on the west bank of the Indus, which circumstance, added to intelligence, that the snow lay still deep on the Peer-Punjal mountains, induced RUNJEET SINGH to suspend his proposed expedition until the following spring. He accordingly sent a detachment to occupy and seize the passes in the hills beyond Rajaoree, and to select places for grain and store-depôts, and then returned, viâ Rohtas, to Lahôr, where he arrived on the 26th of December.

The confiscation of the hill territory of Hureepoor, and its annexation to the Lahôr *Khalsa*, (fisc), was the first act which marked the return of the Sikh ruler to his capital. BHOOP SINGH, the Raja, whose treacherous seizure and confinement preceded the confiscation, received on its completion a small Jageer for subsistence. The next act of RUNJEET SINGH was more shamelessly extortionate. Hearing that SHAH SHOOJA had still some jewels of rare value, a demand was made for them; and, on the Shah's declaring that he had none left, the Sikh determined to judge for himself, and sending BHYA RAM SINGH with a party of females to search the interior apartments, caused to be brought into his presence, every box or packet the Shah possessed. The Shah's head Eunuch was then made to open them, and RUNJEET seized, and retained for himself, all the most precious articles, with the swords, pistols, and two cart loads of carpets, and women's dresses. The Shah was then ordered to remove from the Shahlemar garden and palace to a common house in the city, and was subjected there to strict surveillance. After experiencing every kind of indignity and discomfort, he determined to attempt an escape with his family. Towards the end of November, it was reported to RUNJEET SINGH, that the Begums of SHAH SHOOJA were missing, whereupon the Shah's person was placed under a guard, and alternate threats and promises were employed to induce him to declare where they were gone. He denied all knowledge of their motions or intentions. The city was searched, and egress forbidden to all veiled women, and all merchants having property of the Shah's, or of any members of his family, in deposit, were ordered to surrender it into the Sikh treasury. These precautions were, however, taken too late. It was ascertained that the Begums had left the house of SHAH SHOOJA in the dress of Hindoo females, and thence had been conveyed to the banking house of BALUK RAM, the agent or correspondent of SOOGUN CHUND, a great banker at Dehlee, and treasurer of the British Residency there; that by him they had been assisted in passing out of the city, and provided with the means of making their way to Loodeeana, where they had arrived safely, and making themselves known to Captain BIRCH, the Assistant, in temporary charge of the station, were received with hospitality and attention. BALUK RAM was seized by RUNJEET SINGH for the part he had taken in this evasion, and was compelled to show his books, and render up all property in his possession belonging to the Shah or his family. He received, however, no further punishment.

In April 1815, SHAH SHOOJA himself made his escape in disguise from the close confinement in which he was held. His guard was disgraced, and a reward offered for recovery of the prisoner, but the Shah succeeded in reaching the hills, where he was hospitably received by the petty Raja of Kishteewar. Here he collected a body of 3000 men, and in the winter season made an attempt on Kashmeer : but the cold prevented his passing the Peer-Punjal range, and his troops dispersed. His condition was now desperate, but after a long and circuitous journey over the Kooloo mountains with few attendants, and fewer comforts, he at last, in September 1816, joined his family at Loodeeana, and placed himself under the protection of the British Government. A provision of 50,000 Rs. per annum was assigned for the maintenance of the Shah in his exile, while he might remain in the British territory. With the intermission of one unfortunate enterprize, he was led to engage in for the recovery of his lost power, after the murder of FUTEH KHAN in 1818, he has since continued to avail himself of this asylum, and he has been joined at Loodeeana by his sightless brother SHAH ZUMAN, whom, with his family already in abject poverty, RUNJEET SINGH took no trouble to detain. To this prince a separate allowance of 24,000 Rupees per annum has been assigned. The chronological order of events has been somewhat anticipated, in order to bring the misfortunes of these princes into one connected relation. The first expedition of RUNJEET SINGH against Kashmeer will take us back into the year 1814. The events, however, which preceded or attended it, will more fitly form the subject of another chapter.

CHAPTER SEVENTH.

A. D. 1814 to 1818.

First expedition of Runjeet Singh against Kashmeer. Fails. Failure of Runjeet Singh's health. Expedition against, and capture of, Mooltan. The army deprived of its plunder. Death of Futeh Khan, Vuzeer of Kabool. Runjeet Singh's advance to Peshawur.

RUNJEET SINGH having celebrated the Hoolee and bathed at Umritsur, moved his army in April 1814, into the Hill country about Kangra, to enforce the collection of his tributes, and the personal attendance of the Rajas with their contingents. Having thus strengthened himself with a large body of hill-men, he moved to Bhimbur on the 4th June; and, advancing slowly from thence, was met by AGUR KHAN, the chief of Rajaoree, through whose territory lay the route to Kashmeer. On the 11th June, the army arrived at Rajaoree, and disencumbering itself of heavy baggage, equipped itself for mountain movement, preparatory to the passage of the famous Peer-Punjal range. An attempt had been made to gain the Poonch Raja, ROOH-OOLLAH KHAN, to the Sikh cause, but he pleaded engagements with Kashmeer, and the presence of his son as a hostage with UZEEM KHAN, the governor. After a consultation of the principal officers however, it was determined, nevertheless, that the main army, commanded by RUNJEET SINGH in person, should pursue the Poonch route, and endeavour to penetrate by the Toshu Mydan pass, while a strong diversion should be made by Buhramgulla towards Soopyn in the valley.

The cavalry being dismounted, and every man furnished with provisions for three days, a detachment was formed, and sent forward on the 15th June, under RAM DYAL, a grandson of MOHKUM CHUND Dewan, with whom were DUL SINGH and other Jageerdars. They appeared before the post at Buhramgulla on the 18th, and after a little negociation, obtained possession of the pass, on payment to the defenders of the arrears due to them by the Poonch Raja. Heavy rain set in on the 20th June, and the Sikh army beginning to suffer from the wet and cold, and the supplies already running short, the march of the main body was delayed until the 26th. On the 28th, however, RUNJEET SINGH reached Poonch, and found it evacuated; the Raja having given orders to his people to attempt no resistance in arms, but to desert their towns and villages, to bury or remove the grain, and to hover in small parties on the flanks of the invaders. The consequences of this system had already begun to be felt, and compelled a halt at Poonch for further supplies, until the 13th July. Thence advancing by Mundee,

RUNJEET SINGH reached Toshu Mydan on the 18th, where he found MOHUMMUD UZEEM KHAN with the forces of Kashmeer, drawn up to oppose his progress. The Sikh army took up its position in face of the enemy, and remained for some days inactive. Here RUNJEET SINGH received intelligence from the detachment at Buhramgulla. On the 19th July, RAM DYAL and the Jageerdars ascended the Peer-Punjal mountains, by the Suraee and Mudpoor pass, driving before them the Kashmeer troops left to defend it. RUNJEET SINGH was uneasy at this precipitancy, thinking his detachment out of reach of support, and liable to be overpowered; he sent off immediately therefore a reinforcement under BHYA RAM SINGH. The Rajaoree chief recommended an attack of UZEEM KHAN, as the best means of preventing his undertaking any thing against the detachment, but RUNJEET SINGH having reconnoitered the position, deemed the attack too hazardous. It is probably the only thing that would have prevented the disasters which followed.

In the mean time RAM DYAL having passed the mountain barrier, and debouched upon the valley at Heerapoor, was attacked on the 22d July, by a party sent against him by UZEEM KHAN. The Kashmeerian, were defeated, and followed to Soopyn. On the 24ths RAM DYAL assaulted the town: but it was well defended by SHOOKOOR KHAN, and the assailants were repulsed, whereupon the Sikhs retired again to the Peer-Punjal mountains to wait reinforcements. BHYA RAM SINGH, hearing of this discomfiture, deemed it necessary to halt at Buhramgullee, with the support he was bringing up, in order to secure the pass.

MOHUMMUD UZEEM KHAN seeing matters in this critical position, thought the time favorable for offensive operations against the main army, which had already suffered much from sickness, and more from desertion. On the 29th July, ROOHOOLLAH KHAN, the Poonch chief, approached, and commenced a desultory fire on the Sikh position. On the following morning he renewed his attack with more vigour, and RUNJEET SINGH was compelled to fall back on Mundee. Being pursued thither, he fired the town, and directing his disciplined battalions to cover the retreat, continued his retrograde march to Poonch, which he reached on the 31st July, with the loss of many men, and his principal officer MIT-SINGH BUHRANEEA, and stripped of nearly all his baggage. The army was now no longer in a state of organization or discipline, and setting fire to Poonch, RUNJEET SINGH quitted the camp and continued his flight to Bhoohee, whence he with a few attendants took the nearest route to Lahôr, which he reached on the 12th August.

RAM DYAL and the Jageerdars serving with him in the detachment which had penetrated into the valley, were surrounded, and their supplies were cut off, but the detachment was allowed by UZEEM KHAN to retire, and was furnished with a safe conduct to the Sikh frontier, in consideration of the friendship professed by this Governor for Dewan MOHKUM CHUND, its commandant's grandfather. That distinguished officer of RUNJEET SINGH had himself been prevented by indisposition from taking part in the expedition. He warned his master however of the difficulties he must expect if he allowed himself to be overtaken in the hills by the rainy season, and particularly pointed out the necessity of providing large depôts in Bhimbur and Rajaoree, in anticipation of a determined opposition from the Moosulman chief, and the whole population of Poonch. All had happened exactly as he predicted, and the ruler of Lahôr returned to lament the deprivation of his Dewan's experience and judgment, no less than his tried skill and valour, in this important expedition. The illness however which prevented him from accompanying the Sikh army increased, and in the course of October, soon after the return of RUNJEET SINGH to Lahôr, he died amidst the regrets and lamentations of all well-wishers to the power of the Sikhs, and to the dominion of RUNJEET SINGH. In his private character the Dewan was liberal, upright, and high-minded: he enjoyed the confidence of the troops placed under his command, and was popular and much respected amongst the entire Sikh community.

The losses sustained by RUNJEET in this expedition required some time to repair. The Sikh army was not therefore in a condition to take the field at the close of the Dussera of 1814 as usual: but in April 1815, a force was employed, under RAM DYAL and DUL SINGH, ravaging the Mooltan and Buhawulpoor territories, and exacting tributes and contributions in that neighbourhood. RUNJEET SINGH himself passed the hot weather at Adeena-nugur, raising and disciplining new battalions; and especially recruiting men of the Goorka nation, of whose valour he began to entertain a very high opinion, from having watched the operations, which during the season had passed in the hill country east of the Sutlej. The British Government had engaged in hostilities with the Goorkhas, and Colonel, afterwards General OCHTERLONY, had taken the field there against UMUR SINGH, who for six months, maintained himself at Ramgurh and Maloun, and baffled the known skill and the superior forces of this experienced commander. His final discomfiture, and the dispossession of the Goorkhas from all the hill territory west of the Gogra or Kalee river, occasioned a breaking up of their power, which was highly favourable to RUNJEET'S views, and procured him many men of this nation particularly well adapted for hill warfare.

In the mean time, the defeat of the Sikh expedition against Kashmeer encouraged the Moosulman Chiefs of Bhimbur and Rajaoree to break out into rebellion, and towards the close of the year 1814, the son of the latter who was detained as a hostage at Lahôr, effected his escape and joined his father. The Bhimbur insurgents were headed by the brother of SOOLTAN KHAN, who since he made his submission in 1813, had been himself detained by RUNJEET SINGH, and was now a close prisoner at Lahôr.

In October, after the Dussera of 1815, the Sikh army was called out, and its rendezvous for muster appointed at Seealkot. A division was sent in advance under RAM DYAL and DUL SINGH to punish the Bhimbur and Rajaoree Chiefs, and to ravage their territories with fire and sword. Poonch was saved from a similar visitation by its greater elevation, and by the setting in of winter with severity. RUNJEET SINGH was not yet prepared for an attempt to retrieve his fortune and lost reputation, by another expedition against Kashmeer.

He was content therefore to employ the season in confirming his authority in the hills before subdued, and in punishing the disobedient and refractory Rajas and Chiefs on this side the Peer-Punjal range. He returned to Lahôr on the 28th December, where he was waited upon by BEER SINGH, the Rajah of Noorpoor, in the hills, who had failed to attend the summons to rendezvous at Seeal-Kot. A heavy mulct was imposed, which being beyond the Chief's means, he offered his Thakoors, or household Gods, of silver and gold, in pawn, but these not sufficing, he was arrested at the door of the *Durbar*, or hall of audience, on the 20th January 1816, and next day was sent off in a Palkee to witness the seizure and confiscation of his all, and to render an account to the sequestrators. He declined the petty Jageer offered to him for subsistence, and after a fruitless attempt to recover his fortress and territory by force, took refuge within the British territory. A second example was made of the Raja of Juswoul OMED SINGH, for a similar failure. Being stripped of his possessions, however, he accepted the Jageer tendered.

After completing his arrangements in the hills, RUNJEET SINGH having bathed at Turun-Tarun, moved with his army into the territories of Mooltan and Buhawulpoor, where the still unripe crops and abundant herds presented the means of enforcing contributions or inflicting irredeemable injury. The Sikh detachments penetrated down the Indus, to the verge of the Sindh territory, and MOHUMMUD KHAN, Chief of Bhukur and Leeah, of the family ejected by the present Meers of Sindh, having recently died, a demand of tribute was made on his successor HAFIZ AHMED KHAN. On his refusal, his forts, Khangurh and Muhmoodkot, were occupied, and PHOOLA SINGH Akalee was allowed to perpetrate there atrocities and insults to the Mohummedan population of the most revolting description. HAFIZ AHMED soon after paid down a sum of money to procure the withdrawing of the Sikh garrisons, and thus recovered his forts with part also of the plunder extorted. AHMED KHAN of Jhung was now summoned to the presence, and called upon for a large contribution. On pleading inability, he was sent prisoner to Lahôr, while three battalions proceeded to occupy, and annex to the Khalsa, the whole of his possessions, reckoned to yield about four lakhs of yearly revenue. They were farmed to LALA SOOKH-DYAL for 1,60,000 rupees. FUTEH SINGH Aloowala was at the same time employed in seizing Ooch and Kot-Muharaja, the first held by Seyuds, who had hitherto been respected, and were now provided with a Jageer; and the second by a chief named RUJUB ULEE KHAN, who was sent prisoner to Lahôr.

RUNJEET SINGH returned from the south west, and re-entered his capital on the 20th May. Here he learned that the Vuzeer FUTEH KHAN had employed the season in a march across the Pukholee and Dumtour hills, into Kashmeer, where he aided his brother in enforcing the collections, and establishing his authority in the valley, and then returned by the same route. The Sikh detachment under RAM DYAL and DUL SINGH had remained upon the frontier to watch his motions.

A domestic matter now occupied the attention of RUNJEET SINGH. His second wife, the mother of

Koonwur KHURUK SINGH, was accused of scandalous improprieties, and particularly of too notorious and close an intimacy with BHYA RAM SINGH, the Koonwur's Dewan. RUNJEET SINGH had lavished much territory in Jageer upon the heir-apparent, and the management was undertaken by his mother and the Dewan, upon the usual condition of maintaining an efficient contingent of horse, for service with the Sikh army. Complaint, however, was loud and frequent, that the Jageers were the scene of extortion and mismanagement, while the condition and equipment of the Koonwur's contingent was deemed by RUNJEET highly discreditable. He first endeavoured to procure a reform by exciting the pride of his son, who was of age to take an interest in such things, but the influence of the mother and Dewan preventing any amendment, the Sikh ruler was at length compelled to interfere more authoritatively. The Dewan RAM SINGH was thrown into confinement, and ordered to account for his stewardship of the Jageers, and the Koonwur's mother was directed to fix her residence in the fort of Shekhoopoor. KHURUK SINGH was reprimanded for allowing such proceedings ; and BHOOANEE DAS of Peshawur, was assigned to him as a new Dewan. Several lakhs of rupees and some valuable jewels were extorted from RAM SINGH, whose banker OOTUM CHUND of Umritsur, was also called to account, and made to refund what he held for the ex-Dewan.

After the Dussera in October, RUNJEET SINGH'S first journey was into the hills, where he paid a visit to Raja SUNSAR CHUND at Nadoun, and collected his yearly tributes ; thence returning, he effected the confiscation of the Jageers and territories of BEER SINGH and DEWAN SINGH, two brothers of the late JODH SINGH Ramgurheea, valued at five lakhs of rupees yearly revenue. The persons of both chiefs were seized, as they came to the Durbar to pay their respects, without suspicion of any design against them being entertained by the Lahôr ruler. Umritsur was illuminated for the return of its sovereign on the 13th of December.

The constitution of RUNJEET SINGH, though it must have been excellent to have carried him so long through a course of life consisting of alternate toils and debaucheries, each extreme in degree, began now to yield to these incessant trials. His digestion failed, and with loss of strength, thinness of body, and the incapacity for much exertion, were superinduced. Towards the commencement of 1817 his health was seriously impaired, and he submitted to a course of regimen prescribed by his native physicians, which continued for forty days, but produced in the end little permanent benefit. No military enterprize or other active operation is recorded as having been undertaken in this year. The Sikh ruler's principal source of anxiety in the course of it, arose from an attachment to RAM LAL, the brother of his chamberlain, KHOOSHHAL SINGH, upon whom such unlimited bounties had been lavished, and who had become the great court favorite, and the bottle companion of his master. RAM LAL could not be induced by the most seductive offers to give up his Brahminical thread, and adopt the Sikh ritual and customs as his brother had done. In order to avoid further importunity on the subject he fled to his home east of the Sutlej, where he was beyond the reach of the Lahôr ruler, who, provoked that he should have escaped, wreaked a real or pretended vengeance on his chamberlain, by removing him from office, and placing him under restraint. RAM LAL returned for his brother's sake, and ultimately received the *Pahul* or Sikh initiation, and changed his name to RAM SINGH.

The following season was employed in preparation for an expedition against Mooltan, of which the resources had been annually drained by forced contributions, ravage, and waste, so as to lead RUNJEET SINGH to hope that MOZUFFUR KHAN'S means of defence and preparation were now so impaired, as to make the city and fort an easy conquest. Before undertaking this enterprize, however, RUNJEET SINGH gave liberty to AHMED KHAN of Jhung, whom he had held in close confinement for nine months. A small Jageer was assigned to him for subsistence. The Sikh army had been ordered to rendezvous in the beginning of the year 1818 on the south-west frontier of the Sikh dominion. KOONWUR KHURUK SINGH was now appointed to the nominal command, aided by MISUR DEWAN CHUND, who had risen by his merit and activity from a low situation to be Commandant of the Artillery, and who undertook for the reduction of the fort of Mooltan, if vested with the chief command during the siege. The jealousy of the Jageerdars, who objected to serve under a man of yesterday, obliged RUNJEET SINGH to adopt the plan of sending his heir-apparent in nominal command of the whole. All the boats on the Ravee and Chunab were put in requisition to carry supplies and stores for the army, and the march was commenced in January 1818. A demand was made of an exorbitant sum in cash and of five of MOZUFFUR KHAN'S best horses, and this not being immediately complied with, his two forts of Mozuffurgurh and Khangurh were stormed and taken. In the course of February the city of Mooltan was occupied, and its citadel closely invested without much loss. The approaches were made according to no consistent plan, but every Jageerdar and chief erected his own battery, and a promiscuous fire was kept up from guns and small arms against every part of the defences. The means of the garrison were however so deficient, that even under this irregular method of attack, the wall of the citadel was, by the continual fire kept up, breached in several places, and the upper works and defences were nearly demolished in the course of the month of April. In May the approaches were carried close to the *Dhool-kot*, or fausse braye of the works, and the army became eager to be led to the storm; but RUNJEET SINGH, who, though absent, regulated every thing connected with the siege, forbad any risk being run, and continued his offer to the Nuwab of a Jageer if he would surrender. He was obstinate in his refusal, and seemed determined to hold out to the last extremity. While matters continued in this state, an Akalee fanatic, SADHOO SINGH, on the 2d of June, advanced without orders with a few companions, and attacked sword in hand, the Afghans in the Dhool-kot, who, being at the time asleep or negligent, were overpowered. The men in the Sikh trenches, seeing this, advanced simultaneously on the impulse of the moment to support the attack, and the entire outwork was carried with a slaughter of those defending it. Flushed with this success, the assailants attempted the fort, and found ready entrance by the breaches made, the garrison not expecting assault, nor being prepared for a consistent and determined resistance. The citadel was thus suddenly carried, MOZUFFUR KHAN with his four sons, and household, made a final stand at the door of his residence, but fell covered with wounds. Two of his sons, SHAH NUWAZ KHAN and HUQ NUWAZ, were also killed on the spot, and a third was left badly wounded. SURFURAZ KHAN, the fourth, who had been vested by his father with the government under himself, was found in a vault or cellar, and taken prisoner. The citadel was now sacked, and an immense booty fell to the troops engaged in the assault. RUNJEET SINGH, however, was not content, that his treasury should be defrauded of the wealth known to have been laid up in this citadel, and which he had long coveted and hoped to have secured by a surrender on capitulation. He accordingly issued peremptory orders for the immediate return of the whole army to Lahôr, with exception to a detachment, under JODH SINGH Kulseea, of sufficient strength to hold the place, and conduct the local administration. SOOKH DYAL, who had taken the farm of Jhung, as above stated, was nominated to the civil government. Upon the arrival of the army at Lahôr, proclamation was made, that the plunder of Mooltan was the property of the State, and all soldiers, officers, or Jageerdars, possessing any article of spoil, or any money obtained in the sack of the fort, were ordered to bring the same in, and to account for the whole to the treasury, under penalty of heavy mulct or confinement. It affords a strong proof of the awe, in which the power and sources of information possessed by RUNJEET SINGH, were held by his troops, that this order produced no outrage or general resistance. Most of the spoil was traced and collected for the treasury, and, though rendered up with much discontent, and with many efforts at concealment, still the severities practised on the obstinate, and the mutual jealousies and envy of their fellows, felt by those who had been compelled to disgorge, led generally to the discovery of all that was valuable, so that the *Toshuk-khana*, or jewel-office, of the Lahôr ruler, was enriched by this respoliation of the troops. There is but one example of similar audacity in a commander, and that was the terrible NADIR SHAH, who, upon his return from India, when his army was crossing the Attuk, placed a guard at the ferry, and as every one came over, searched his person and baggage, for every article of the spoil of Dehlee, that the soldiers or followers of his army might have secured.

SURFURAZ KHAN and his wounded brother ZOOLFIKAR KHAN were conducted to Lahôr, where RUNJEET SINGH assigned them a small stipend for subsistence. The capture of Mooltan was the only operation of the season, the whole Sikh army having been employed against the place since January, and the rains having set in as it fell. During that season GOVIND CHUND, Raja of Datarpoor, in the hills, dying, his territory was annexed to the Khalsa, and his son was held in durance until he consented to accept a Jageer.

This season of necessary inactivity produced, however, another event of great influence on the future fortunes of RUNJEET SINGH. In the month of August 1818, the Vuzeer FUTEH KHAN, whose energy and talents had raised SHAH MUHMOOD to the throne of Kabool, and who alone kept together the turbulent and discordant materials of which the Afghan empire had been composed, was plotted against by the Prince KAMRAN, the son of

MUHMOOD, and being treacherously seized, was first blinded, and soon after put to death by his order. The Vuzeer had fifty brothers, all at the head of governments, or otherwise in the possession of power and wealth, and the cry to vengeance was general throughout the kingdom. MOHUMMUD UZEEM posted from Kashmeer, leaving a younger brother, JUBUR KHAN, in the valley. Taking the direction of the measures of resistance organized, he defeated the troops of KAMRAN, and dislodged his garrisons from the neighbourhood of Kabool, Ghiznee, and Kandahar, so that in a few months the authority of the weak SHAH MUHMOOD, and his rash ill-advised son, was confined to the city and plain of Herat, and the rest of the Afghan territory was assumed and portioned out in separate governments and independent principalities, by the powerful members of this extensive family. The plea put forward by KAMRAN for his conduct towards the Vuzeer FUTEH KHAN, was, his having plundered the property of FEEROZ-OOD-DEEN, a prince of the blood royal, whom he expelled from the government of Herat, in order to recover it for MUHMOOD. The real cause, however, was jealousy of his power and reputation, and the vain conceit entertained by KAMRAN, that the Vuzeer's abilities could be dispensed with, and affairs conducted as well by the household and family of the imbecile nominal sovereign.

The intelligence of these events determined RUNJEET SINGH to carry his army across the Indus in the ensuing season, more especially as a detachment of Sikhs had recently been overpowered by the Khutuk Moosulmans, and every motive of policy required, that this should not pass unrevenged. The troops having been called out in

October, advanced to Attuk under RUNJEET's personal command, and the river being forded with some loss, the fortress of Khyrabad, with Jugheera, and the territory on the opposite bank, were reduced and occupied. No immediate resistance was offered, FEEROZ KHAN, the chief of the Khutuk tribe, made his submission, and RUNJEET SINGH having ascertained that no organized force was in the field to oppose him, directed an advance on Peshawur. The city was entered on the 20th November, YAR MOHUMMUD KHAN, the governor, retiring, as the Sikhs advanced, into the mountains occupied by the Yoosufzye tribes of Afghans.

RUNJEET SINGH remained with his army three days in Peshawur, and then returned, leaving as governor on his behalf, JUHAN DAD KHAN, to whose treachery he was indebted for the possession of Attuk, but whom he had left unrewarded hitherto, and without the promised Jageer. He furnished him, however, with neither troops, nor money, to maintain the possession. Accordingly, the Sikh army had no sooner crossed the Indus on its return, than YAR MOHUMMUD came down from the mountains with the Yoosufzyes, and expelled the Sikh governor: JUHAN DAD KHAN fled to the southward, and there fell in with SHAH SHOOJA, whom the state of affairs in Kabool had tempted from Loodeeana again to try his fortune. From him he received a free pardon, and joined his standard. The curse of Fate was, however, on every enterprize undertaken by this prince, whose character, though amiable in many respects, and irreproachable in all, possessed not the energy to inspire awe, and attach followers in troubled times, or to give confidence to those disposed otherwise to favor his cause.

SHAH SHOOJA returned destitute to Loodeeana, after a few months of vain wandering, and fruitless negociation with the Meers of Sindh, and other quondam tributaries and dependents of the Afghan empire now no more; and JUHAN DAD KHAN then made his peace with the Court of Herat, and proceeded thither, despairing of obtaining favor or advancement at that of Lahôr.

CHAPTER EIGHTH.

A. D. 1819 to 1822.

Seeond expedition and conquest of Kashmeer. Arrangements for consolidating the Sikh authority in the hills. Conquests on the Indus. Disgrace and confinement of Suda Koonwur, Runjeet's Mother-in-law. Arrival and entertainment of French officers.

In February and March 1819, Desa Singh Mujhiteea was employed by Runjeet Singh, with Raja Sunsar Chund, in collecting the hill tributes. In the course of their operations they came in contact with the Raja of Kuhloor, whose capital, Bulaspoor, is on the British side of the Sutlej, but who held at that time extensive possessions north and west of that river. This chief refusing the tribute demanded, Desa Singh marched to occupy his territory, and having dispossessed him of all he held on the right bank of the boundary river of British protection, sent a detachment across it against Bulaspoor. Captain Ross, the Political Agent in the adjoining hills, and Commandant of a battalion of Goorkha light troops, stationed at Subathoo, marched immediately to the point threatened, and was joined there by a detachment from Loodeeana, ordered out by the Resident at Dehlee. This promptitude alarmed the Sikh ruler, and DESA SINGH was ordered, not only to recall his detachment, but to wait upon Captain ROSS, and offer every explanation and apology in his power.

Nothing material occurred in the early part of this year, but the season was occupied in preparation for a second expedition against Kashmeer. To this RUNJEET SINGH was encouraged, partly by his recent success against Mooltan, which had given him confidence in his troops, and had added largely to their reputation, but mainly by the state of the Afghan power, and the knowledge, that MOHUMMUD UZEEM KHAN had carried with him the most efficient of the troops in the valley, to forward his other designs, and was far absent, and in no condition to render assistance to the Governor he had left behind him. Misur DEWAN CHUND, the conqueror of Mooltan, was selected by RUNJEET SINGH to command the present expedition, the Sikh ruler being influenced, partly by his bodily infirmities, partly by a superstitious notion, that fortune and fate were against his personal success in the valley, but mainly perhaps by the knowledge, that the more important task of expediting supplies, and supporting the armies operating in advance, could best be performed by himself, to determine to remain within his own frontier, and in the plains of the Punjab.

In the month of April, the Sikh army was marched towards the frontier, and a select and strong division was formed there under the Misur's command to lead the advance. A second army was formed to support this officer, and placed under the command of KOONWUR KHURUK SINGH; while RUNJEET SINGH kept with himself a reserve to be employed as occasion might require in expediting stores and supplies.

By the beginning of June, Misur DEWAN CHUND had occupied Rajaoree and Poonch, and all the hills and passes, south of the Peer-Punjal range. The supporting division was accordingly advanced to Rajaoree, to keep open the communications. The Chief of this last place was in rebellion, and acting with the Raja of Poonch in the defence of the Peer-Punjal passes. RUNJEET SINGH, however, had given liberty to SOOLTAN KHAN of Bhimbur, after a confinement of seven years, and had secured the aid of his advice and co-operation, by holding out hopes of extensive benefit to result to him from the success of the enterprize. On the 23d June, the Misur attacked the Rajaoree and Poonch Rajas in their position at the Dhakee Deo and Maja passes, and carried them, thus securing to himself a road over the Peer-Punjal. KHURUK SINGH with his division advanced now to Surdee Thana, and RUNJEET SINGH with his reserves came up as far as Bhimbur, while Misur DEWAN CHUND, crossing the barrier mountains, descended into the valley, and took up a position at Suraee Ulee on the road to Soopyn.

JUBUR KHAN, who had been left by MOHUMMUD UZEEM, Governor in Kashmeer, was at Soopyn with five thousand men, to make his stand for the possession of the valley. The troops he had were however raw, and hastily raised, and unable to compete with the disciplined battalions led by Misur DEWAN CHUND, which besides outnumbered them greatly. On the 5th July, the Sikhs having been furnished with supplies and reinforcements from the rear, the Misur advanced to Soopyn, and immediately on coming in view of the Kashmeer army, ordered an attack, which, after a few hours of smart fighting, attended with considerable loss on both sides, was completely successful. The Afghans and troops of JUBUR KHAN fled at once across the mountains towards the Indus, leaving the valley to be occupied without further opposition by the victorious army of RUNJEET SINGH. Great was the joy of this chief at his success. The cities of Lahôr and of Umritsur were illuminated for three nights, and MOTEE RAM, son of the late Dewan MOHKUM CHUND, was sent as governor of the valley, accompanied by a strong body of troops, for the reduction of Durbund and other strong holds, and with instructions to spare no effort to bring the Poonch and Rajaoree chiefs to accept terms and make their submission.

The arrangements, consequent upon the subjugation of Kashmeer, occupied RUNJEET SINGH for the remainder of the year 1819. Towards its close, the Sikh army was again called out, and led by RUNJEET SINGH in person to Mooltan, whence operations were directed for ravaging the territories of the Nuwab of Buhawulpoor, and southward as far as Bhukur, belonging to the Meers of Sindh, with a view to extort augmented tribute and contributions. Dera Ghazee Khan, on the west bank of the Indus, was at the same time wrested from its Governor, ZUMAN KHAN, and, in the settlement made with the Buhawulpoor chief, the place was given to him in farm at a heavy rent.

RUNJEET SINGH returned to Lahôr in April, 1820, bringing with him a horse of high repute, that he had extorted from Hafiz AHMED KHAN of Munkèra. Many subsequent enterprizes were undertaken for similar animals; the love for them, and the desire to possess all of any repute for excellence, being a growing passion carried by the Sikh chief almost to folly. The horse acquired in this instance, bore the name of *Soofed-Puree.*

In Kashmeer the troops were employed in petty operations against isolated chiefs. One of these, SHEER ZUMAN KHAN of Gundgurh, having risen in rebellion, RAM DYAL, the governor's son, and the hopeful grandson of the late Dewan MOHKUM CHUND, was employed against him, and unfortunately met his death in an action, that took place, which was a source of deep regret to RUNJEET SINGH, no less than to his father MOTEE RAM, and of general sympathy with all; for he was a rising officer of great promise in the Sikh army. The Raja of Rajaoree, AGUR KHAN, was in the course of May seized, and made prisoner by GOOLAB SINGH, brother of MEEAN DHEEAN SINGH, the *Deohreewala,* or Lord of Privy Chambers, of the Lahôr Court. For this service, the family obtained in Jageer, the principality of Jummoo, with which they had long been connected. In June, the troops employed in Kashmeer, having suffered much from sickness, were relieved, and the Governor MOTEE RAM, who was of pacific devotional habits, was changed for a more martial chief in the person of HUREE SINGH Nalooa, a Sikh Jageerdar, who had killed a tiger single-handed on horse-back, with the sacrifice, however, of his horse.

In this season, the Court of Lahôr received two visitors, one the ex-Raja of Nagpoor, MOODAJEE BHOOSLA, commonly called APA SAHEB, who escaped as a fugitive, and in disguise, after the campaign, which ended in the capture of Aseergurh, and which finally reduced the last Mahratta opponent in arms of the British Supremacy in India. The fugitive resided some time at Umritsur, while RUNJEET SINGH was with his army to the south-west, but on this chief's return, he was required to quit the capital and dominions of the Sikh, whereupon he retired to seek refuge in the hills with Raja SUNSAR CHUND. There, engaging in some intrigue with the Kabool Princes at Loodeeana, he was required by the Raja to leave his court, whereupon he proceeded to Mundee, where the chief EESHUREE SEIN gave him temporary protection. The British Government, though aware of the locality of this fugitive's residence, made no demand for his person, and troubled itself no further, than to obtain information of his proceedings and designs.

The other visitor was the Superintendent of the Company's Studs in India, the adventurous traveller Mr. MOORCROFT, who passed through Lahôr, on his route to Ludak, as a merchant proceeding to purchase horses in Bokhara. He was received with much civility and attention by the Sikh, and from Ludak, which he reached viâ Mundee, made good his route across the northern mountains into Kashmeer. Thence descending into the plains he went to Bulkh, and met his death, by fever, in a rash attempt to pass a tract of unhealthy country, of the malaria of which at the particular season, he was fully forewarned, but relied too confidently on his European remedies, and on his own medical skill.

After October the muster of the Sikh army was taken at Seeal-kot, whither RUNJEET SINGH proceeded by the route of Buttala. Thence, skirting the hills, and sending detachments against the turbulent Chib-Bhao tribe to ravage their possessions; he proceeded to Rawul Pindee, and dispossessing the chief, NUND SINGH, annexed it to the Khalsa. RUNJEET SINGH returned to Lahôr on the 13th December, and for the rest of the season was occupied chiefly in domestic arrangements.

SHEER SINGH, the eldest of the children brought forward by SUDA KOONWUR, had been adopted, and brought up by her with great expectations. He was now approaching man's estate, and began to be clamorous for a Jageer, and separate establishment. RUNJEET SINGH himself encouraged him in this, hoping that the Ranee would make a provision suitable, from the possessions of the Ghunee Sirdaree in her management. She, however, desired to force the recognition of the young man, and the making provision for him, on RUNJEET, who was obstinate in refusing. The wily Sikh fomented the dispute between SHEER SINGH and his adoptive mother, and gained over BYSAKH SINGH, an old and highly confidential retainer of the Ghunees, who was in great trust with SUDA KOONWUR. After this intrigue had been carrying on for some time, and SHEER SINGH's complaints had made their impression, unfavorable to SUDA KOONWUR, RUNJEET SINGH thought matters ripe for an authoritative act of interference on his part. He accordingly sent to his mother-in-law an order, in October 1820, to set apart half of her own Jageer for the suitable maintenance of the two youths SHEER SINGH and TARA SINGH, whom she had brought up with such high expectations. She remonstrated against the order in vain, and being herself in the Sikh camp, then pitched at Shah-Dehra, and consequently in the power of RUNJEET SINGH, she felt the necessity of complying so far, as to execute a deed making the assignment required. But she had no sooner done so, than she plotted the means of escape, and after a time left the camp secretly in a covered carriage. Intelligence of her evasion was conveyed to RUNJEET by BYSAKH SINGH. DESA SINGH was accordingly sent with a detachment of horse to bring her back, and she was committed by her son-in-law's order to close confinement. Not content with this punishment, RUNJEET SINGH ordered a division of his army to march and sequester all her wealth and territory, and this was effected, after a resistance of a few weeks by one of her female attendants, who was in charge of the fort of Uttul-gurh, her principal strong hold. Thus, after an influence, maintained for nearly thirty years, fell at last this high-spirited woman. She had been serviceable to RUNJEET SINGH, indeed, was the main stay of his power, in the early part of his career, and it was through her intrigues, and with her aid, that RUNJEET was able to assume authority so early, and to put aside his Mother and her Dewan. The independence she asserted, and the high tone she was accustomed to assume, had for some time been irksome to the Sikh ruler in his growing fortunes, and her ruin was prepared by the course of events, no less than by her own unbending disposition. She bore the restraint of her confinement with great impatience, continually beating her breast in lamentation, and venting imprecations on the head of her ungrateful son-in-law.

Another domestic event which in the time of its occurrence somewhat preceded the catastrophe of SUDA KOONWUR'S fall, was the birth of a son to KOONWUR KHURUK SINGH. The event took place in February 1821, and was the occasion of great festivity and rejoicing; the child was called NOU-NIHAL SINGH. In April, RUNJEET moved to Adeenanugur, and remained there till July, occupied in collecting the hill tributes. The two petty territories of Kishteewar and Man-Kôt, were in this interval, annexed to the Lahôr Khalsa. The harshness of HUREE SINGH having made him unpopular and obnoxious to the inhabitants of Kashmeer, he had been removed again in December 1820, and the mild and peaceable MOTEE RAM was now re-appointed governor.

The above events having occupied the hot season and rains of 1821, the Sikh army was called out as usual after the Dussera, and RUNJEET SINGH taking the command in person, led it to the Indus, into the possessions of the Chief of Munkèra, Bhukur, and Leea, south of Mooltan. Annual contributions and forced presents had for some time been habitually extorted from HAFIZ AHMED, the Nuwab: it was determined to reduce and assume possession of the whole of his country. With this view, the army marching by Ram-Nugur, Noor-Meeanee, Pind-Dadur-Khan, and Bheera-Khooshab, reached the Indus at Meeta-Thana, and on the 5th November, was encamped opposite to Dera-Ismaeel-Khan. A detachment of 8000 men was sent across, and the place was surrendered on the 9th by MANIK RAEE. Bhukur, Leeah, Khangurh, and Moujgurh, were then all successively reduced without resistance. Munkèra, fortified with a mud wall, and having a citadel of brick, but protected more by its position, in the midst of a desert, was now the only stronghold remaining. It was situated amongst sand hills, in which there was a difficulty of supplying a besieging army with fresh water. A division was advanced for the investment of this place on the 18th, and Beeldars were set to dig wells, and seek every where for water, the troops being supplied in the first instance, at great expense and trouble by land conveyance of this necessary from Moujgurh, on camels, ponies, or bullocks. By the 25th November, wells sufficient having been sunk, a further division was advanced to complete the investment of the place, and RUNJEET SINGH moved there himself soon after, with his head-quarters, to superintend the conduct of the siege. Each Jageerdar as usual was allowed to conduct his own approaches, and an active rivalry and spirit of competition was kept up amongst them by RUNJEET SINGH. Between the 26th November, and the 6th and 7th of December, the besieger's works were carried close to the ditch of the place, but not without suffering from the continual fire of the besieged. The Nuwab HAFIZ AHMED, conceiving that enough now had been done for his honor, proposed terms, and stipulated for the surrender of Munkèra, under condition of his being allowed to march out with his arms and personal property, and of receiving the town of Dera-Ismaeel-Khan, with a suitable Jageer. RUNJEET SINGH granted the terms, and desired to be put in possession of one of the gates of the fort. Solemn pledges were exchanged, and rich dresses sent to the Nuwab, and every means taken to allay his suspicions. On the 14th December 1821, he admitted a Sikh detachment, and surrendered the gates to it; and on the 18th, he came out with 300 followers, and encamped at a spot assigned to him within the Sikh position. On the 20th, he waited on RUNJEET SINGH, and was received with marked attention. An escort was sent with him to Dera-Ismaeel-Khan, and the treaty, as a new example of Sikh faith, was observed to the letter, and fully executed. An engagement for tribute was now enforced on the Balooch Moosulmans of Tonk and Sagur west of the Indus, and the Sikh army then moved to Dera-Deen-Punah. RUNJEET SINGH here embarked on the Indus, sending his army by land to Mooltan. At Dera Ghazee Khan, he arranged with the Nuwab of Buhawulpoor for an increase of tribute, and of rent upon the farms he held of that place, and Mitteen Kôt. On the 10th January 1822, he rejoined his army at Mooltan, but on the 16th posted on to Lahôr, leaving it to follow. On arrival at his capital on the 27th, he learned that one of his principal Sirdars and Jageerdars, JY SINGH Utareewala, had gone over to the Afghans west of the Indus.

It was in March of the year 1822, that the first European adventurers presented themselves at RUNJEET SINGH'S Durbar, seeking military service, and entertainment. There arrived in that month two French officers, one Monsieur VENTURA, an Italian by birth, and the other Monsieur ALLARD. Both had left Europe to seek their fortunes in the East, upon the death blow given at Waterloo, to the hopes of the military youth of France. They had since been employed in Persia, but liking not the subordinate place they were there required to fill, they made their way after a time, through Kandahar, and Kabool, to Lahôr. RUNJEET SINGH was at first very suspicious of their motives, and could not at all understand what could have induced two young men to leave their native country, and travel so far. He could not believe, that employ in his service was a sufficient object to have induced such a journey. They had stated their views verbally, and had besides given several representations in Persian, but these failed to satisfy the suspicious chief. He accordingly desired them to write down their views and wishes in their own language, and having thus obtained a paper in the French language, RUNJEET sent it to his Agent at Loodeeana, to be there literally translated for him*, and returned. On obtaining

* The French paper referred to, was to the following effect.

A SA MAJESTE LE ROI.

SIRE,—Les bontés dont votre Majesté nous a comblés depuis notre arrivée en cette capitale sont innombrables. Elles correspondent à la haute idée que nous nous etions faits de l'excellence de son bon cœur ; et la renommée, qui a porté jusqu' à nous le nom du Roi de Lahôr, n' a rien dit en comparaison de ce que nous voyons. Tout ce qui entoure votre Majesté est grande, digne d'un souverain, qui aspire à l'immortalité. Sire, la premiere fois que nous avons eu l'honneur d'être presentés à votre Majesté, nous lui avons exposé le motif de notre voyage. La reponse qu'elle a daignée nous faire nous tranquillise; mais elle nous laisse dans l'incertitude pour l'avenir. C'est pour ce motif que nous avons eu l'honneur de faire, il y a déjà quelques jours, une addresse a votre Majesté, pour savoir si notre arrivée dans ses etats lui etait agrèable, et si nous puissions lui être de quelque utilité par nos connoissances de l'art de la guerre, acquises comme officiers superieurs sous les ordres immediats du Grand Napoleon Bonaparte, souverain de la France. Votre Majesté ne nous a pas tiré de l'incertitude, puisque nous n'avons pas encore rien d'ordres de sa part. Nous avons donc renouvellé notre demande en langue Francaise d'après le conseil de NOOR-OOD-DEEN Saheb, qui nous fait croire qu'un employé auprès de votre auguste personne connoit notre langue. Dans cette incertitude nous supplions votre Majesté de daigner nous faire transmettre ses ordres, que nous suivrons toujours avec la plus grande ponctualité.

Nous avons l'honneur d'être, avec le plus profond respect,

Sire,

De Votre Majesté les très humbles, très obéissans

et très devoués Serviteurs,

CH. VENTURA. CH. ALLARD.

Lahôr, 1*st April*, 1822.

this satisfaction, RUNJEET SINGH gave to the two French officers assurance of employ; and houses in Lahôr, with handsome salaries, were at once assigned to them. Monsr. VENTURA was an Infantry Colonel in the French service, Monsr. ALLARD had similar rank in the Cavalry. They were both set to instruct troops in the European method of exercise and manœuvre. The native commandants were at first extremely jealous of the favor shown to these Europeans, and of their exercising any authority or command; more especially because on RUNJEET SINGH'S asking their opinion of the troops in their present condition, they had expressed themselves very slightingly as to their state of discipline and drill. At first they were employed on the troops at the capital, which were under RUNJEET'S own eye, and Monsieur ALLARD received orders to raise a corps of Dragoons, to be disciplined and drilled like the Cavalry of Europe. These officers by their conduct won further confidence in the course of time, and some others, particularly Monsieur COURT, who was brought up at the Polytechnic Institution at Paris, have followed, and joined them in subsequent years. VENTURA is now (1833) employed with upwards of 10,000 men in a separate command of importance towards Mooltan, and there is a perfect confidence and good understanding between him, and those serving under him. The feeling is, however, still so adverse to Europeans on the part of the Sirdars, as to make the situation of these officers very hazardous and delicate in the event of RUNJEET SINGH'S decease. Monsieur VENTURA, moreover, in 1829, had a quarrel with the heir-apparent, KHURUK SINGH, which was with difficulty adjusted, and the consequences of which will be likely to be felt injuriously when this prince shall succeed his father.

Towards the beginning of April, RUNJEET SINGH went to Ukhmur, in the Jummoo hills. His army was in the field, under MISUR DEWAN CHUND, watching the movements of UZEEM KHAN, who had come down to Peshawur; where being joined by the fugitive Jageerdar, JY SINGH Atareewala, he was pushing back the Sikh posts and garrisons towards the Indus, and even threatened Khyrabad, the principal station held by them on the western bank. In June, RUNJEET returned to his capital, without achieving any enterprize of note.

Amongst the possessions of SUDA KOONWUR, was a small territory, called Himmutpoor Wudnee, lying south of the Sutlej, and held by her under grant from RUNJEET SINGH, made in September 1808, in consideration of a payment of 15,000 rupees. This territory being on the protected side of the Sutlej, could not be confiscated with the rest. RUNJEET SINGH, however, compelled his mother-in-law to execute in his favor, a deed of relinquishment of right to the territory, and armed with this, his agent proceeded to take forceable possession. Upon resistance, however, by SUDA KOONWUR'S manager, and complaint to the British authorities, this deed was at first not admitted as valid, and the lands were ordered to be left in the former management. They continued thus to be preserved from the grasp of the Lahôr ruler, until 1828, when upon further representation, the Supreme Government consented to RUNJEET SINGH'S assuming them under his management. SUDA

Koonwur's position was not in the least improved by this result. She continued, and to this day (1833) continues, to be held a close prisoner, and howsoever humanity may plead in her behalf, one does not see how she could well be treated otherwise, being what she is, and has been.

CHAPTER NINTH.

A. D. 1823 to 1831.

Operations in Peshawur. Affair with a party of Moosulman fanatics. Mohummud Uzeem Khan retires and leaves Peshawur to Runjeet Singh. Death of that Chief—also of Sunsar Chund. Disturbances in the Gundgurh Mountains. Yar Mohummud confirmed as Governor for Runjeet Singh at Peshawur. Futeh Singh Aloowala retires from the Durbar. Rise of Seyud Ahmed, the Mohummedan Saint and reformer, troubles occasioned by him. Unrodh Chund of Kangra moved to a discreditable alliance, flies across the Sutlej. His possessions seized. Further disturbances and troubles from Seyud Ahmed. His defeat and death.

In October, after the Dussera of 1823, the Sikh army was assembled at Rohtas, and muster taken of the Jageerdars' contingents. Runjeet Sing was on this occasion more than ordinarily severe in taking account of the numbers, and equipment of the men produced, and amongst other chiefs, who fell under his animadversion for neglect, was Dul Singh Mihèrna, an old Jageerdar, who had served with much zeal and honor. He was threatened with a heavy mulct, and in other respects treated disparagingly; whereupon he took poison at night, and so relieved himself from further troubles. The army moved, in December, towards Rawul Pindee, whence Hukeem UZEEZ-OOD-DEEN was sent forward to Peshawur, to demand tribute from YAR MOHUMMUD KHAN the Governor. This chief, being unprepared for resistance, collected some valuable horses, and forwarded them as tribute, which satisfying RUNJEET SINGH for the time, he returned to his capital in January, making the pilgrimage of Kitas on his route.

MOHUMMUD UZEEM KHAN disapproved of the compromise made by his brother of Peshawur, and marched from Kabool to superintend the affairs of this quarter in person. He arrived at Peshawur on the 27th January; and YAR MOHUMMUD, fearing to meet him, sought a temporary refuge in the Yoosufzye hills. RUNJEET SINGH now ordered his army to cross the Indus, and the the river was forded on the 13th March. FEEROZ KHAN, the chief of the Khutuks, being dead, a sequestration was made of all his possessions. On the 14th March, the army entered Akora, where it was joined by the fugitive, JY SINGH Utareewala, who was now anxious to make his terms, and be re-admitted to favor. His pardon was granted. Intelligence was soon after brought, that MOHUMMUD ZUMAN KHAN, nephew of UZEEM KHAN, with SUDEEQ KHAN, son of the deceased Khutuk chief, FEEROZ KHAN, were in position at Noushuhur near the camp, with about 4000 men, and had already cut off some parties of foragers. RUNJEET SINGH ordered his army to be formed, directly he learned this intelligence, and marched forthwith to attack the Moosulmans. The battle commenced with a furious charge led by PHOOLA SINGH Akalee, a Sikh desperado, who was in the habit of rushing forward, with some followers of like zeal, at the commencement of action. The Moosulmans, however, also felt their battle to be a religious one, and met the fanatic Sikhs with corresponding zeal and bigotry ; so that the latter were completely destroyed, and their leader slain. Fresh troops were now ordered up by RUNJEET SINGH, but the Mohummedans stood firm, and resisted every attack until sunset, by which time they had lost nearly half their originally small number, but still maintained their ground on two insulated hills. RUNJEET SINGH now ordered his cavalry to surround the whole position of the enemy, and directed his Nujeeb and Goorkha battalions, to charge and dislodge them. Twice did these troops advance to the charge, and twice were they repulsed by the determined body opposed to them, nor could the utmost efforts of RUNJEET'S army dislodge them from their position before nightfall. In the course of the night, the remnant of the band cut their way through the surrounding posts of the Sikhs, and so made good their retreat to the mountains.

There were not more of the Moosulmans engaged on this occasion, than between four and five thousand men, and these were mere mountaineers and villagers, who turned out for the *Ghazee*, that is, to fight the religious battle against the infidel Sikhs. Disciplined professional soldiers there were none amongst them, yet did they resist, for a whole day, the entire army of RUNJEET SINGH, who had in the field against them not less than

24,000 men, and all his best troops. There were upwards of 1,000 men (Captain WADE says 2,000) killed and wounded on the side of the Sikhs, and amongst them four officers of distinction, PHOOLA SINGH Akalee, GHURBA SINGH, and KURUM SINGH Chahul, two Jageerdars, and BULBHUDUR SINGH Goorkhalee. The last named was the officer who had defended Nalapanee, with so much determination, against Generals GILLESPIE and MARTINDELL, at the commencement of the British war with Nipal. After peace was re-established, he formed an ill-fated connexion with the wife of another, and, by the law of Nipal, his life became forfeit to the injured husband. This led to his expatriating himself, and taking employment from RUNJEET SINGH, where, after serving with distinction, he died in a manner worthy of his reputation.

MOHUMMUD UZEEM KHAN was, during this action of the *Ghazee*, or fighters for the faith, at Chumkawa, about four miles and a half east of Peshawur. He made no effort to succour, or support the warriors, and was watched in his position by a Sikh force under KRIPA RAM, SHEER SINGH, and HUREE SINGH, which had advanced by the opposite bank of the river. Upon learning that the party was overpowered, and had dispersed, he retired himself to Julalabad on the Kabool road, leaving the field clear to RUNJEET SINGH and the Sikh army.

On the 17th March, RUNJEET SINGH made his entry into Peshawur, and advanced the army to Khybur Durra, where it was employed in pillaging and destroying the cultivation. It suffered much, however, from the activity and bigotted spirit, with which the Moosulman population attacked its parties, and cut off all stragglers; and the camp was kept during the night continually on the alert by their daring skirmishes.

In April, RUNJEET SINGH secured the submission of YAR MOHUMMUD KHAN, who came with some fine horses, including the far-famed Kuhar, and with a request to be allowed to hold Peshawur as a tributary of Lahôr. The Sikh was well content to make a settlement for the city and surrounding territory on this basis. Having effected it, he returned to his capital in person on the 26th April.

MOHUMMUD UZEEM KHAN died in the following month, and the event contributed to produce further confusion in the affairs of Afghanistan; for while he lived, he was looked upon as the head of the family in succession to FUTEH KHAN, whereas after his death the numerous brothers and nephews of that chief acknowledged nobody, and their quarrels and contentions covered with outrage and disturbance, all the fairest portion of the Afghan territory. MUHMOOD and his son KAMRAN were confined to the fort and city of Herat, beyond which their name was no where respected, nor could they exercise any authority.

After the Dusserah, in October, the Sikh army being again called out, was led by RUNJEET SINGH down the Indus, with the professed design of an attack upon Sindh. The river was crossed in November, and the whole of that month was occupied in reducing Bhutee villages, and exacting contributions from the Balooch and other Jageerdars, whose possessions lay on the extreme northern frontier of the Sindhian territory. The Lahôr Chief was however content with having thus felt his way this season, and in December moved his army homeward. At the close of the year Raja SUNSAR CHUND of Kangra died, and was succeeded by his son UNRODH CHUND. A Nuzurana was demanded on the succession; and, upon the young Raja demurring to the payment, RUNJEET SINGH summoned him to attend in person at his summer residence of Adeenanugur. He was persuaded by the FUQEER UZEEZ-OOD-DEEN to obey the summons, and met the court at Juwala Mookhee. On arrival, an exchange of turbands took place, and mutual pledges were interchanged, between him and KHURUK SINGH on the part of the Durbar; and, after much negociation, a lakh of rupees was at last settled, and paid, as the Nuzurana of accession, by UNRODH SINGH.

HUREE SINGH Nulowa, who had been left with a force to overawe the turbulent Moosulman population of the mountains about Gundgurh and Durbund, contrived by several harsh and vexatious proceedings, and particularly by the seizure of a Seyud's daughter of beauty, and credit in her tribe, to drive the whole into insurrection. The insurgents collected in such force, as to compel HUREE SINGH to stockade himself, and remain on the defensive, and he wrote to RUNJEET SINGH, representing the difficulties of his situation, and soliciting reinforcements. RUNJEET ordered him to put on a bold face, and maintain himself as he could, but sent no immediate reinforcements, indeed the rains had set in, and it was not easy to do so. HUREE SINGH in the mean time being attacked, suffered a severe loss, and was compelled to retire before the insurgents. The Sikh army was in consequence of this disaster, called out earlier than usual, and directed against the hills between the Indus and Kashmeer, in the early part of October. By the 19th, RUNJEET had penetrated with a division of his troops to Gundgurh, but found the population dispersed, and nothing but empty walls and deserted houses; the place with all the surrounding villages was burnt and pillaged, the unripe crops were used for forage to the army, and RUNJEET SINGH following the deserters, determined to ford the Indus after them, an attempt in which many lives were lost, but the object was effected on the 3rd November. When the army was well across, MOHUMMUD YAR KHAN was summoned to attend from Peshawur, which after some hesitation he did on the 16th November, bringing a present of horses, which were at first rejected, as of inferior quality, but, being replaced by others, the offering was accepted, and the terms on which Peshawur had been assigned were renewed with fresh protestations and oaths of allegiance on the part of the Afghan chief. On the 30th November, the Sikh army re-crossed the Indus, not without further loss, from the depth and bad footing at the ford. On the 10th December, RUNJEET SINGH re-entered his capital by no means satisfied with the result of the expedition of the season, for he had incurred heavy expenses in preparation, and yet had been able to inflict no blow on the turbulent body of Mohummedans in insurrection, and had levied very little in the way of tribute and contribution. No further expedition was attempted in 1824, nor in the early part of the following year. Indeed the Burmese war had been commenced by the British Government, and RUNJEET SINGH seemed to watch with intense interest all the events and operations of it. The most exaggerated reports were spread at first of the successes of the Burmese, and there were not wanting counsellors to instil into the ear of the Lahôr ruler, that the time was approaching, when the field would be open to him to the east. It was at this period, that Mr. MOORCROFT forwarded to Calcutta, a letter of Prince NESELRODE, the Russian Minister for Foreign Affairs, addressed to RUNJEET SINGH, purporting to introduce an agent named AGHA MEHDEE. The agent it seems was endeavouring to make his way by the difficult route of Tibet, and either died, or was murdered, some few stages from Ludâk. There Mr. MOORCROFT obtained his papers, and amongst them this letter, which he procured to be translated afterwards by M. KSOMA DE KOROS, with whom he fell in on his travels. The letter, except as introductory of the agent, was merely one of compliment, with assurances of protection to any merchants of the Punjab, who might penetrate to the Russian dominions.

No Military enterprize was undertaken in the season 1824-1825: but, towards April 1825, sequestration was made of all the Jageers and possessions formerly assigned to Dewan MOHKUM CHUND, and now managed for MOTEE CHUND by KRIPA RAM, the Dewan's grandson. The bad management of the Jageers, and the inefficient contingent kept up by this agent, were the assigned reasons, MOTEE RAM himself being left in his government of Kashmeer, and subjected to no indignity, or diminution of favor, consequent upon the sequestration. In the Dussera of 1825, the army was called into the field, with the avowed purpose of an expedition against Sindh. With this view, RUNJEET SINGH marched the troops to

Pind-Dadur-Khan, but learning there, that the Sindh country was suffering from scarcity and famine, he gave up the design, and returned to Lahôr on the 24th November. An agent he had sent into Sindh to demand tribute, returned with Vakeels from the ruling Meers, who for some time continued to reside at Lahôr. It was at this period that RUNJEET SINGH'S close associate hitherto, and turband brother, FUTEH SINGH Aloowala, conceived some suspicions as to the safety of his position at the Lahôr Durbar, and suddenly left that capital to place himself in security within the possessions held by him on the protected side of the Sutlej. RUNJEET SINGH was much vexed at this sudden step of his old ally, and made great efforts to induce the chief to return, and resume his place in his Durbar. The British officers, while they confirmed him in the assurance of the inviolability of his territory on the protected side of the Sutlej, advised his not yielding to vague suspicions, as a ground for breaking a friendship of so long standing, as had subsisted between himself and RUNJEET. Guided by this advice FUTEH SINGH some time after, that is, in April 1827, yielded to the invitations of the Lahôr ruler, and returning to his Durbar was well received, the Maha Raja sending his grandson NOU-NIHAL, to give him the meeting of honor. He soon, however, became an object of rapacity, being called upon to pay tribute, or take in farm at no easy rent, much of the territory he had hitherto enjoyed free, by the assignment of his turband brother.

The year 1826 passed without any military enterprize or event of importance. SADIQ MOHUMMUD KHAN, the Nuwab of Bahawulpoor, died in April, and was succeeded by BUHAWUL KHAN, the present Nuwab, who renewed his father's leases and engagements with RUNJEET SINGH, for the territory he held west and north of the Sutlej. In September, a question arose upon the application of QOOTUB-OOD-DEEN of Kasoor to be received under British protection, as holder of Mundot and Rumnawala on the left bank of the Sutlej, but the feudatory relations this chief had come under to RUNJEET SINGH for these, as for his other possessions, forbad the British Government from holding out the hope that he could be received under protection as an independent Chief. An unsuccessful attempt by BEER SINGH, Ex-Raja of Noorpoor, in the Hills, to recover the territory, from which he had been ejected since 1816, forms the only other event recorded in this year. He was defeated and made prisoner by DESA SINGH. A main cause of the inactivity of the Sikhs arose from the increasing infirmities of RUNJEET SINGH: His indispositions and ailings increased upon him so much, towards the end of the year, that he applied to the British Government for a medical officer, and Dr. ANDREW MURRAY was sent over from Loodeeana to attend his Highness.

It was in the early part of 1827, that the reformer SEYUD AHMED, raised the green standard of Mohummud in the Mountains inhabited by the Yousuf-Zyes, and commenced a religious war against the Sikhs. This individual was originally a petty officer of horse in the service of AMEER KHAN. Upon the breaking up of the military establishment of that Chief in 1818-19, SEYUD AHMED took a fanatic turn; and fancying he had received special revelations, went to Dehlee, and associated himself with some Mooluvees of sanctity of that city. One of them collected these revelations into a book; and from it the SEYUD, and his associates, and followers, commenced preaching against many irregularities that had crept into the practise of the Mohummedan religion. Amongst the principal were, the reverence paid by the Mooslims of Hindoostan to the tombs of saints and relations, the manner of their celebrating the death of HUSUN and HOOSEIN, the sons of ULEE, and other similar customs, which these reformers denounced as idolatrous, and as deviations from the pure precepts of the Koran. In 1822, SEYUD AHMED came down to Calcutta, and was there much followed by the Moosulman population. Thence he took ship to make the pilgrimage of Mekka. On his return, he travelled through Hindoostan, and declared the intention of devoting himself to the service of his religion, by waging an interminable holy war against the Sikh infidels. Many zealots and fanatics joined him, and subscriptions of money were poured in upon him from all parts of the British possessions. Thus armed and prepared, he made his way to the hills near Peshawur, and raised the Mohumdee Jhenda as above stated amongst the Yoosufzye Moosulmans. RUNJEET SINGH was compelled by the formidable character of the insurrection thus organized, to send a strong force across the Attuk, for the protection of Khyrabad and his interests in that quarter. In the month of March 1827, the SEYUD at the head of a countless irregular host, ventured to attack this force, which was commanded by BOODH SINGH Sindoowaleea, and had thrown up works to strengthen itself in its position. The Sikh discipline and superior equipment secured them an easy victory, and the SEYUD, being entirely defeated, retired with his followers into the hills, whence he kept up a desultory and annoying warfare with the Sikhs, directed against their convoys and small detachments.

Lord AMHERST passed the hot season of the year 1827, at the station of Shimla, near Subathoo, in the hills east of the Sutlej. The proximity of this position to Lahôr induced RUNJEET SINGH to send a mission of compliment to His Lordship, with presents, and amongst others a handsome tent of shawl for the King of England. The mission was received with distinction, and a return compliment made of the same kind. Captain WADE, the officer at Loodeeana, through whom the correspondence with the Lahôr ruler was conducted, and some officers of the Governor General's personal suite, were deputed to Lahôr with return presents, and a suitable retinue, to express the Governor General's satisfaction at the terms of cordiality and friendship, which subsisted between the two states. In 1828, the British Commander in Chief, Lord COMBERMERE, passed the warm season at Shimla, and a complimentary Vakeel was sent over by RUNJEET SINGH, to offer his congratulations. It was his Lordship's desire to procure an invitation in person to Lahôr, but the wily Chief evaded compliance with this wish.

At the Durbar of Lahôr, at this time, the entire favor of the Chief was engrossed by Raja DHEEAN SINGH, the Chamberlain, and his brothers GOOLAB SINGH and SOOCHET SINGH, Meeans of Jummoo, where their influence had been re-established under RUNJEET SINGH's authority, by the grant of the place in Jageer in 1819, as before related. HEERA SINGH, a boy of about twelve years of age, son of Raja DHEEAN SINGH, was the object of particular favor, RUNJEET SINGH seldom suffering him out of his sight, and seeming to delight in humouring all his whims and caprices. In common with his father and uncles, he was created Raja, and RUNJEET SINGH studied to procure him a high matrimonial alliance. It was about this time that Raja UNRODH CHUND, son of SUNSAR CHUND of Kangra, paid a visit to Lahôr, with his family, on his route to attend the nuptial ceremonies of the Aloowala's son, NIHAL SINGH. He had with him two sisters, on whom Raja DHEEAN SINGH cast his eyes, desiring them to be joined in matrimony with his family. The pride of the hill chief was roused at the proposition of so degrading an alliance, but the influence of RUNJEET SINGH procured from him a written promise, that the two young women should be at his disposal. The mother of UNRODH CHUND, however, succeeded in carrying them off, and took refuge with them in the hills under British protection, whither UNRODH CHUND himself soon followed, leaving his possessions on the other side of the Sutlej at the mercy of RUNJEET SINGH, who sequestered the whole, and received the surrender of them without any resistance from FUTEH CHUND, UNRODH'S brother. A *Khawas* or concubine of Raja SUNSAR CHUND, named GUDDUN, was enticed away from the family, and fell on this occasion into RUNJEET SINGH'S hands, with several children she had borne to the late Raja. Two of the daughters the Sikh married himself, and upon a son he conferred the title of Raja with a considerable Jageer. The nuptials of HEERA SINGH were at the same time celebrated with great pomp, though not with a member of the Kangra family.

In the course of 1829, SEYUD AHMED again appeared in the field in great strength, and his vengeance was directed against YAR MOHUMMUD KHAN, who, he declared, had sacrificed the cause of his religion by swearing allegiance, and accepting service from the Sikhs. As the SEYUD approached Peshawur, YAR MOHUMMUD moved out with such troops as he could collect for its defence. In the action which followed, however, he received a mortal wound, and his troops dispersed. Peshawur was saved to RUNJEET SINGH by the opportune presence there of Monsieur VENTURA, who had gone with a small escort, to negoc̀iate with YAR MOHUMMUD KHAN for the surrender of a famous horse called Lÿlee. The horse had been demanded in the previous year, but the Afghans declared it was dead. The falsity of this declaration being discovered, a written engagement had been extorted from YAR MOHUMMUD, pledging himself for its delivery, and Monsieur VENTURA was deputed to enforce the execution of this deed. Upon the death of YAR MOHUMMUD, he took upon himself to make dispositions for the defence of Peshawur, and wrote to RUNJEET SINGH for instructions as to his further proceedings. The Sikh directed the city to be delivered over to SOOLTAN MOHUMMUD KHAN, brother of the deceased YAR MOHUMMUD, but urged the securing possession of the famous horse Lylee, as an indispensable preliminary. Monsieur VENTURA succeeded fully in this negociation, and brought away Lylee, leaving SOOLTAN MOHUMMUD in possession of the government of Peshawur.

M. VENTURA had not been long gone, when SEYUD AHMED appeared again, with his host of YOOSUFZYES, before Peshawur, and SOOLTAN MOHUMMUD, venturing an action, was defeated, so that Peshawur fell under the temporary power of the fanatic Chief. RUNJEET SINGH took the field with his army in the early part of 1830, to punish this pretender. On his crossing the Attuk, however, and approaching Peshawur, the insurgent force dissolved before him, and nothing tangible appeared on which he could wreak his vengeance. He returned to Lahôr, leaving a strong detachment across the Indus, to act as occasion might offer, and having restored SOOLTAN MOHUMMUD to his government. This Chief, after the departure of RUNJEET SINGH, found it convenient to come to terms with SEYUD AHMED, who again came down, and by a sudden attack carried Peshawur. The Governor consented to allow free passage to men and money proceeding to join the reformer—to place the administration of justice in Peshawur in the hands of a Kazee, and officers of the reformed faith and principles, and to pay monthly to the Seyud the sum of 3000 rupees. The city was on these conditions restored to SOOLTAN MOHUMMUD, but the Seyud had no sooner retired, than the Kazee and two Moolvees left to administer justice according to his reformed principles, were slain in a popular tumult. SEYUD AHMED'S difficulties increased, for the Yoosufzyes took offence at some innovations he desired to introduce into the marriage ceremony, and were alarmed by his announcing the doctrine, that a tenth of all income, or revenue, should be subscribed for religious and state purposes. The wild untutored mountaineers rose against the preacher's authority, and not only rejected these doctrines, but compelled the Seyud, and his immediate followers, to leave their mountains. He fled across the Indus, and found a temporary refuge in the mountains of Pekhlee and Dhumtour. RUNJEET SINGH, however, sent a detachment against him, under SHEER SINGH, and in the early part of 1831, the detachment was fortunate enough to fall in with him, when after a short, but smart engagement, the Seyud's force was dispersed and himself slain. His head was cut off, and sent in to be recognized and identified. His followers in Hindoostan have, however, difficulty in believing yet, that he is dead; and still hope to see him revive in energy, and display himself in some great action, for the permanent benefit of the faith of MOHUMMUD, and for the extension of the dominion and power of its professors.

Since the death of the Seyud, the neighbourhood of Peshawur has been comparatively tranquil, and there has been no occasion to call out the Sikh army, nor has RUNJEET SINGH engaged in any military enterprize of importance.

CHAPTER TENTH.

A. D. 1829 to 1831.

Mission of Lieutenant Burnes with a present of dray horses for Runjeet Singh. His journey through Sindh, and up the Indus and Ravee to Lahôr. Mission to Lord William Bentinck at Shimla. Meeting arranged between the Governor General and Runjeet Singh. Takes place in October 1831. *Commercial Treaty concluded between the British Government and Sindh.*

WHEN Lord AMHERST returned to Europe in 1828, he carried with him the shawl tent presented by RUNJEET SINGH to the King of England. It was determined to send from England a return present, and a very extraordinary selection was made; upon whose advice, has not transpired. It was resolved to send to RUNJEET SINGH, on the part of His Majesty, a team of cart horses, four mares and one stallion, upon some conception, that, in his love for horses, RUNJEET SINGH must be a breeder of the animal, and would be well pleased to have mares of large size to cross with the breeds of the Punjab. The fact, however is, that RUNJEET has no breeding stud nor establishment, and cares only for entire horses of high courage, well broken in to the manége of Hindoostan, that he can ride himself, on parade, or on the road, or set his choice sirdars and favorites upon. The result fully showed this, for when the cart horses arrived at his court, the stallion was immediately put into the breaker's hands, and taught the artificial paces usual. This animal with its enormous head, and coarse legs, stands always in the palace yard, or before the tent of the chief, decorated with a golden saddle, and necklaces of precious stones, and is sometimes honored by being crossed by RUNJEET SINGH himself. The mares are never looked at, and are matters of absolute indifference to the Sikh. It is, however, an anticipation to state what happened on the arrival of the animals, their adventures on the road to Lahôr, involved matters of higher interest.

It was resolved to make the transmission of this present, a means of obtaining information in regard to the Indus, and the facilities, or the contrary, it might offer to navigation. The recent successes of Russia in Persia, and the probability of that power entertaining further designs, either present, or hereafter, when the succession of ABBAS MEERZA to the throne of Persia, might render that kingdom a province of Russia, made it desirable, that every intelligence should be collected, as to the frontier states of India, and the means of defence offered by this great river barrier in particular. The dray horses were accordingly sent out to Bombay, and the Supreme Government instructed Sir JOHN MALCOLM, the Governor of that presidency, to take measures to have them forwarded under charge of an intelligent and prudent officer, in boats up the Indus. Some demur was anticipated on the part of the rulers of Sindh to allowing them passage through the Delta and lower part of the river, but it was assumed that the governing Meers, situated as they were relatively to RUNJEET SINGH on one hand, and the British Government on the other, would not readily incur the risk of offending both powers, by refusing a passage altogether, if it were insisted upon.

Sir JOHN MALCOLM, having received the horses, forwarded them to Kuchh, and appointed to the Mission to Lahôr, in charge of them, Lieutenant BURNES, the Assistant to Colonel POTTINGER, who was in Political charge of that district and of the British relations with Sindh. The young officer thus selected had been in the Quarter-Master General's Department, and was in every respect qualified for the duty. With him was sent Ensign LECKIE, as a companion, and to take the charge, in case of any thing happening to Lieutenant BURNES. Sir JOHN MALCOLM added to the dray horses the present of a carriage of his own, as useless an article to RUNJEET SINGH as the mares. The highly ornamental carriage sent to him by Lord MINTO in 1810, after being used for a few days as a novel plaything, had ever since remained neglected in the great arsenal at Lahôr. The carriage and horses, however, being laden in appropriate vessels, were dispatched from Kuchh towards the end of the year 1830, and Sir JOHN MALCOLM thought the most politic course would be, to send them without previous notice or correspondence with the Meers of Sindh, thinking the necessity they would thus be under of deciding suddenly, would be likely to contribute to the success of the expedition.

Lieutenant BURNES accordingly started, carrying with him the letters announcing the purpose of his coming, and entered with his fleet one of the mouths of the Indus. Passing up to the first inhabited town he forwarded his dispatches to Hydurabad. After a detention of some days, he was, on the 1st February, met by an officer and guard from Darajee, who requested him to wait at the mouth of the river, till orders should arrive from Hydurabad. With this he complied, but there experienced so much incivility from the Kurachee people, who relieved the guard from Darajee, that he resolved to return and wait in Kuchh till the Meers should decide upon his coming. The reply of the Meers to the applications made for this purpose being delayed beyond reason, Lieut. BURNES sailed again for the Indus, and entered the Pyteeanee mouth of that river. Permission to land being still refused, and even fresh water being withheld, Lieut. BURNES found it necessary again to retrace his steps, and was nearly lost in a storm, which scattered his fleet, and drove the vessel which carried himself upon the bar at the mouth of the Pyteeanee. The month of February was lost in these fruitless attempts to penetrate. The objections of the Meers seemed to be insuperable. They were at this time founded mainly on the alleged difficulty of the navigation, and on the distracted state of the country between Sindh and Lahôr, both of which were greatly exaggerated, in order to dissuade Lieut. BURNES from attempting the route by the river Indus. The mission having returned to Kuchh, as above stated on the 23d February, Colonel POTTINGER opened a correspondence with the Meers, and sent an agent to Hydurabad to endeavour to overcome the repugnance shown to letting it pass through Sindh. He made light of course of all that was stated of the difficulty of navigation, and of the dangers from the unsettled state of the country; and pointed out that the horses and bulky carriage could not by possibility be forwarded in any other way than by water, so that it would be a most unfriendly act to both Governments to refuse a passage. The season of 1831 was fast wearing away, and there was still delay in the Council at Hydurabad, in making up its mind on this important matter. A strong letter however of Colonel POTTINGER at last convinced the Chiefs, and MEER MOORAD ULEE, the ruler of the country, in particular, that permission for the horses, and other articles of presents, to pass up to Lahôr, could not in decency, and without giving offence, be refused. The requisite leave was accordingly forwarded, and Lieutenant BURNES sailed again on the 10th March, and on this occasion entered the Ruchel mouth by Kurachee Bundur, the extreme western channel of the river. Here difficulties were made, and delays interposed, so as to induce Lieutenant BURNES to start by land for Hydurabad, in the hope of removing them by personal negociation. He had proceeded no further than Tatta, when after much chicanery he received the required permission to pass by the route of the Indus. Boats of the country were now furnished to him, and every possible assistance rendered for his conveyance to Hydurabad, no effort being spared to obliterate the effects of the previous unfriendly treatment he had experienced. At the capital he was received in Durbar with great distinction, a chief of rank was appointed to attend him on his journey, and the best accommodation-boats on the river, even those of the ruling Meer himself, were assigned for his conveyance. Every where in Sindh he met with the same attention, and proceeded on his voyage by Tatta to Hydurabad, and thence after a short stay to Bhukur, making his observations as the boats leisurely proceeded. The Mission reached Tatta on the 15th, and Hydurabad on the 18th April, 1831, and the month of May had closed before it left the Indus, and entered the Chunab. The river was then at its lowest, but no where was there the slightest difficulty, or obstruction to the navigation.

It may be necessary to state, that Sindh is divided into three independent Governments: the first, and by far the most considerable, is Hydurabad, ruled at this time by MEER MOORAD ULEE, last survivor of the four brothers, who, in 1780, effected the revolution, which transferred the dominion of the country to the present Talpoor Meers. The second division is that of Khyrpoor, to the north of the first, and lying on both sides of the river Indus. Its present ruler is MEER ROOSTUM KHAN, the eldest son of MEER SOOHRAB KHAN recently deceased. The third division is that of Meerpoor, lying towards Kuchh, and ruled by MEER ULEE MOORAD KHAN. These sub-divisions of the country, had their origin in a partition made amongst the principal conspirators, by whose exertions the Talpoorees obtained power.

Having passed through the Hydurabad territory, Lieutenant BURNES was received with even increased attention and kindness by the ruler of Khyrpoor, who professed a strong desire to cultivate a more intimate relation with the British Government, and made Lieutenant BURNES the bearer of a communication to this effect to the Governor General. By this chief the mission was carried forward to the territory of the Nuwab of Buhawulpoor, without experiencing the smallest obstruction or difficulty of any kind: there was found no where less than eight feet water, and the current was moderate, and easily overcome, even where from rocks, or hard soil at the banks, the water-way was contracted. The month of May was now passing, during which the navigation of the Ganges is much obstructed by strong westerly winds, and by the want of water, but no difficulty of the kind impeded the passage up the Indus at this season. The Buhawulpoor chief was already in political relation, both with RUNJEET SINGH and with the British Government: from him therefore Lieut. BURNES was sure of receiving every kindness. On the 30th May, the fleet reached Mittunkot, and embarking on other boats provided by the chief of the Daoodpootras (BUHAWUL KHAN) entered the Chunab, or as it is sometimes called the Punjnud, being the united stream of the waters of the Punjab. A little below Mooltan, the escort and party sent by RUNJEET SINGH to receive and conduct the Royal* present, met Lieutenant BURNES with boats of the Punjab, adapted to the navigation of the winding Ravee. In these Lieutenant BURNES and his party embarked on the 12th June, and soon reached Mooltan. The mouth of the Ravee is further up the Sutlej, and he did not enter that branch till the 23d June. The rainy season overtook the Mission while in that river,

* It is a singular circumstance, that Sir J. MALCOLM in all the instructions he gave Lieutenant Colonel POTTINGER and Lieutenant BURNES in regard to this Mission, never mentioned, nor gave the smallest intimation to either officer, that the dray horses were a present from the King of England. They made the discovery after the difficulties in respect to the passage through Sindh had been overcome, when a direct correspondence with the Mission was opened by the Governor General. Up to this time, they had believed, and had represented the present to be sent from the British Government in India.

and the progress up it was tedious in the extreme, being dependent entirely on the track rope.

On the 17th of July, Lieutenant BURNES reached Lahôr, where his arrival with the present from the King of England, and with the letter of Lord ELLENBOROUGH which accompanied it, was a source of great pride and rejoicing to RUNJEET SINGH. The attention he paid to Lieutenant BURNES was very marked, and he had invited Captain WADE over from Loodeeana, to assist at the ceremonial of reception. From Lahôr, Lieutenant BURNES proceeded to Shimla, to render to the Governor General an account of his mission, and to lay before his Lordship the valuable information obtained during it. This enterprizing and zealous officer obtained His Lordship's permission, to return to his presidency of Bombay through Persia, and to explore the route of Bulkh and Bokhara, after first crossing the Punjab and Kabool territory, in order that he might be the means of adding information of this little known route, to the stores of intelligence already contributed by him.

The very favorable disposition in which the ruler of Lahôr seemed to be at this juncture, encouraged Lord WILLIAM BENTINCK to hope, that a proposition for a personal meeting between himself and RUNJEET SINGH would be likely to be well received. He accordingly instructed Captain WADE, when at Lahôr, on the occasion above related, to sound the Chief's confidential advisers on the subject. As anticipated by His Lordship, the Ruler of Lahôr showed great desire for the meeting, but some difficulty was at first started in respect to the etiquette of a previous return mission, RUNJEET

SINGH having paid his Lordship the compliment of sending one, similarly composed to that which waited on Lord AMHERST. The mission had been received by Lord WILLIAM BENTINCK in April, soon after his arrival at Shimla: its members were the Dewan MOOTEE RAM, son of MOHKUM CHUND, HUREE SINGH Sirdar, and the secretary, Fuqeer UZEEZOODDEEN. They had been treated by the Governor General with much distinction, and a return mission of some of the principal officers of His Lordship's suite had been promised, or rather held out in expectation. The personal meeting between the heads of the two states would necessarily deprive RUNJEET SINGH of this compliment; for in the first place, the time would scarcely allow of both, seeing that the intended journey of the Governor General to Ajmeer and Rajpootana required, that, if arranged at all, the interview should take place before the end of October, and in the second, if a formal mission were sent, immediately before the meeting, it would have the appearance in the eyes of the world, of being sent to supplicate, or induce the ruler of the Sikhs to come to the interview, whereas the rank and position of the Head of the British Government required, that the honor of a personal conference with him should be sought.

With a liberality, not inconsistent with his general character, RUNJEET SINGH, having made up his mind to the interview, gave up the point of etiquette, and preparation was made on both sides, for the meeting to take place on the Sutlej about the 20th of October, without any previous return mission: the neighbourhood of Roopur was subsequently fixed upon as the most appropriate and convenient spot for the meeting.

In order to give the requisite èclat to the occasion, and to form a suitable escort, the Governor General ordered up to Roopur from Meerut and Kurnal, two squadrons of European lancers, with the mounted band of the regiment, (H. M. 16th Lancers,) an European Regiment (H. M. 31st Foot) two battalions of Native Infantry (the 14th and 32d,) and eight guns of horse artillery, also two squadrons of Colonel SKINNER'S Irregular Horse. The escort was thus composed, in order to exhibit to RUNJEET SINGH, whose curiosity was much excited as to the formation and equipment of the various arms and corps of our military force, as much variety as possible. In marching the Europeans through the Sikh territory, the population was somewhat scandalized at ascertaining, that beef was killed in camp for their rations. The slaughter was made in the night, as secretly as possible, still the fact transpired, and became matter of complaint from the Sikh Sirdars. The reply to them was, that it was no business of theirs to enquire what was done within the precincts of a British camp, that our customs prevailed there, and these could not be yielded to their scruples, though every care should be taken to prevent the obtrusion of any thing that was offensive. There is no doubt that the prejudices of the Sikhs were much outraged by the slaughter of oxen, but it would have been extremely bad policy to yield the point in this instance; for were it conceded, and the necessity to arise hereafter of bringing a considerable force of Europeans into the country, similar concession would be expected when it would be impossible to grant it, and the population would be excited, from the want of previous knowledge and preparation for the thing, as a necessary evil attendant on the march of Europeans, no less than by the recollection, that heretofore the concession had been made to their religious feelings.

The troops having arrived at Roopur, the Governor General, who had left Shimla on the 19th October, and in descending took the opportunity of making an excursion in the Hills with few attendants, entered the camp on the evening of the 22d. RUNJEET SINGH came into his camp, on the opposite side of the Sutlej, on the morning of the 25th, escorted by 10,000 of his best horse, and about 6,000 trained infantry. He was immediately waited upon by a deputation from the Governor General, headed by Major General RAMSAY, brother to the Commander in Chief, Lord DALHOUSIE, and by his Lordship's Principal Secretary. KOONWUR KHURUK SINGH, with six principal Sirdars of the Sikhs, came at the same time to present the Muha-Raja's compliments to the Governor General. It was arranged, that RUNJEET SINGH should visit the Governor General next day in the morning.

As the time approached for the meeting, RUNJEET SINGH began to entertain apprehension, that some treachery or foul play must be designed: late over night, he sent to Monsieur ALLARD to say, that he should not attend the meeting of the morrow. Monsieur ALLARD waited upon him immediately, and exerted himself to remove these suspicions, and restore confidence, offering to stake his own head, that nothing would happen that was disagreeable. He left the Muha-Raja still irresolute, and the astrologers were summoned. They consulted the Grunth, and declared the result favorable, but told His Highness to take with him a couple of apples, and to present them to the Governor General and to his Secretary: if they were at once taken without demur, he was to consider it as a good omen, and might proceed in full assurance, that the result of the meeting would give him satisfaction. On the morning of the 26th October, a deputation went to conduct the Muha-Raja to camp, and he started at sunrise. A bridge of the flat-bottomed ferry boats of the Sutlej had been constructed for the convenience of communication. RUNJEET SINGH made to cross over before him, 3000 of his best Gorchur cavalry, dressed in new yellow silk quilted coats, also about 800 of Monsieur ALLARD's dragoons; he then took his breakfast of a highly spiced cordial, and sent over the chiefs he meant should attend on their elephants. This occupied some time, for the boats were fragile and would allow but few elephants to be on the bridge together. Lastly, His Highness passed over in person, and then, to prevent all confusion, ordered the guard at the bridge to permit none else from his camp to cross over. With the escort and attendance thus formed, the Sikh Chief crossed the open plain, at the further end of which lay the camp of the Governor General, from the centre of which a street was formed of the British troops collected. On reaching the end of the line, the Muha-Raja stopped to examine each corps, and put an infinity of questions as to their equipment, asking the use and cost of every strange article, that caught his eye. In the middle of the street he was met by the Governor General, and presented the apples, as enjoined by the astrologers: they were freely and at once taken. His Highness then crossed into the Governor General's houda, and the two Chiefs proceeded together to the tents of audience that had been prepared. In an outer tent, all the European gentlemen were collected, and RUNJEET SINGH was detained in it a short time, that several of them might be presented to him, standing, as he passed through. In a further tent chairs were laid out, and the Muha-Raja, with the chiefs of his nomination, and some select officers of the suite, was led thither by the Governor General for a more private conference. It was amusing to see the pains taken by RUNJEET SINGH in the arrangement of his part of the ceremony. He waited at the door of the outer tent, and himself called, and told off, the chiefs that were to proceed to the inner, making them precede himself in order to prevent confusion or crowding. They were all like himself dressed in yellow, that and light green being the favorite colours of his court, and called *Busuntee*, or the colours of spring. Some wore elegant highly polished armour, with scarfs of this colour, and the splendour of the attire of all was very striking. The inquisitive, and apparently frank manner of the Sikh Chief, made the conference pass off with more liveliness than is usual on such occasions of ceremony. Presents of every variety of manufactured stuffs, which had previously been sent for, from Calcutta, Dacca, and Bunarus, with guns and jewels of value, a fine Burmese elephant, and two select thorough-bred young horses from the Hissar stud, were laid out, or passed in review before his Highness. Dresses of honor, and presents were also laid out for the heir-apparent, and other chiefs, according to a list obtained from his Highness. The Muha-Raja examined carefully every article of his own present, and then sent for the keeper of his wardrobe, and desired him to receive charge, and pack up the articles forthwith. He took his leave, apparently highly pleased with the interview, and at the door of the tent, called up, and paraded before the Governor General, his own favorite horses, telling the names, and merits of each. Again, as he passed through the street of troops, he stopped to examine the different corps, and his enquiries into every minute particular were renewed. It was noon, before he reached his own camp in returning.

On the following day, the Governor General returned the visit, and was met at the bridge of boats by RUNJEET SINGH. His Lordship was escorted by the Lancers, who, with their mounted band, preceded the cavalcade. RUNJEET SINGH was much struck with their appearance, particularly with that of the Band; and, after they had crossed, and drawn up on the farther side of the river, he went up to them, and listened for some time to their playing, while the suite crossed. The Sikh troops formed line, from the bridge to the Muha-Raja's tents, which, consisting chiefly of *Kunâts* and *Shumeeanas*, tastefully arranged, were of red color, and covered a large space. The lining of all the Shumeeanas, under which the chairs were placed for the Governor General and his suite, was of shawl, beautifully worked, and that, under which sat the Governor General and His Highness himself, was a sheet of inlaid pearls and jewels of great value. The Muha-Raja, after the party were seated, introduced his chiefs in succession, and each as he came forward, presented Nuzurs of Dutch gold sequins, both to his Highness and to the Governor General. The horses were again brought forth, and exhibited in superb trappings, and after an hour passed in lively conversation, the presents for the Governor General were laid out, and His Lordship took his leave.

Evening entertainments were afterwards exchanged, and reviews held of the troops collected on both sides. The Muha-Raja seemed particularly struck with some of the evolutions exhibited before him by the British Regiments, and sent his Sirdars up to the ranks, to examine particularly how they were executed. He himself also went up to the squares formed by the Infantry, to see how many ranks knelt, and how many kept up fire, showing in all things a most insatiable curiosity.

On the 31st October, the last day of the interview, the Muha-Raja came across the river, to witness some artillery practice with grape and spherical-case shot. His astonishment at the effect on the curtain at different distances, from four hundred to one thousand paces, was extreme. After amusing himself afterwards with firing at a chutur, or umbrella, with one of the six pounders, and exhibiting feats of horsemanship, and dexterity, by his Sirdars, he was presented by the Governor General with two nine pounder horse artillery guns, with horses, and equipments complete.

The evening of this day, was that of the parting interview, which it was arranged was to take place at the entertainment given by the Governor General. At RUNJEET SINGH'S particular request, a paper was executed, and delivered to him on this occasion, promising perpetual friendship from the British Government. A complete model of an iron suspension bridge, made up at Calcutta for the purpose, was also presented to his Highness, and excited his applause and admiration. On the following morning, viz. the 1st November 1831, both camps broke ground, and commenced their march in

to face page 166

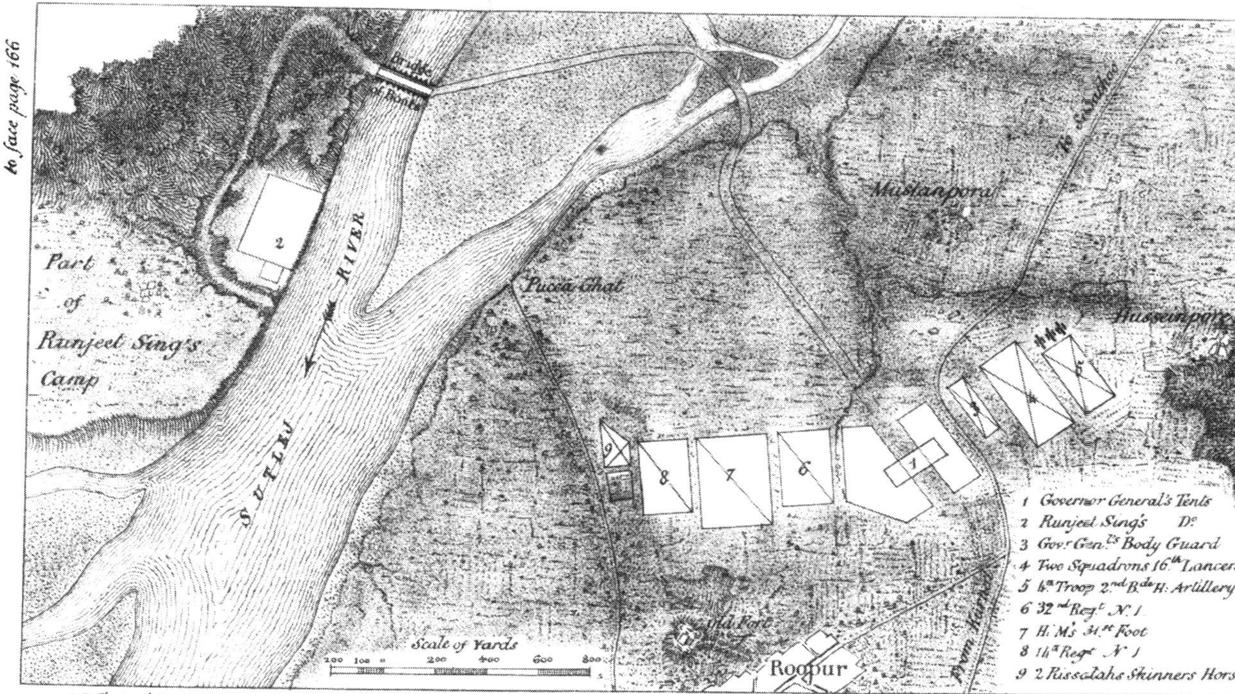

J. B. Tasvin lith.

opposite directions, after a week of magnificence and mutual display, reminding one of the days of "the field of cloth of Gold."

No business of importance was transacted at this interview: RUNJEET SINGH, however, invited the two officers he thought most in the Governor General's confidence to his tent, and in the midst of much desultory conversation, put to the official secretary, who was one of them, several questions in respect to Sindh, as if desirous to open a negociation, and concert measures, in relation to that state; or at least to come to an understanding, as to the views of the British Government in respect to it. He said the vukeels of Sindh were in attendance in his camp, and he asked if he might introduce them to the Governor General. Upon being answered in the affirmative, he added, that it was a very rich country, and much treasure had been accumulated there, ever since NADIR SHAH'S invasion of Hindoostan, that there was no standing army, and no soldiers, except the population at large, who would be called from the plough to take the field against an invading force. He then made allusion to the Meers having sent back Lieutenant BURNES, and to their general character for pride and haughtiness. It appeared evident that the Muha-Raja had learned, or at least suspected, that the British Government had some further views in respect to Sindh; also, that nothing would be more gratifying to him, than to be invited to co-operate in an attack upon that state. Notwithstanding however the desire thus shown, to come to an understanding on the subject, it was not thought advisable to make any communication yet to the ruler of Lahôr; for it was conceived, that, if made aware of the intentions of the British Government, he might, with every profession of a desire to forward them, contrive by intrigue and secret working to counteract the negociation.

On the very day before His Highness arrived at Roopur, instructions had been issued to Lieutenant Colonel POTTINGER to prepare for a mission to Sindh, with a view to the negociation of a commercial treatry, having for its object, to open the navigation of the Indus to the trade of Europe, and of India. The negociation was to be separate with each of the three independent Meers, but Colonel POTTINGER was directed to proceed first to Hydurabad, to arrange with MEER MOORAD ULEE, for a free passage for vessels, and merchandize, through the mouths, and Delta of this great river. The basis of the negociation was to be, to obtain guarantees against the levy of irregular duties, or wanton obstruction of any kind to boats and merchandize, to offer a guarantee against loss of revenue to the Sindh Government from the adoption of the scheme, and so to procure, that the river Indus should become again the channel for extensive commerce, and be frequented securely by the craft and vessels of all the adjoining districts, and even of Europe. The object of entering upon this negociation, at the particular juncture, was perhaps in some measure political, having reference to the necessity of being prepared against the possibility of designs on the part of Russia, should she succeed in establishing her influence in Persia. The Governor General, however, was not prepared to make any avowal or display of such motives, and a commercial treaty, stipulating for the free navigation of the river, seemed to him the better form in which to open relations with the Governments and Chiefs who occupied its banks.

The main argument, however, against treaties of this description is their tendency to lead to embarrassing discussions, and to produce irritation, and acrimonious feelings, while the views acted upon by the British Government are not properly understood by the Chiefs. The whole of Sindh is held in Jageers by Chiefs, who claim to be, and are *de facto*, independent, exercising almost sovereign authority in their respective domains. These Sirdars will not readily be brought to respect boats and merchandize, passing through their possessions, but detention will take place on the plea of examination, and presents will be expected, or forced purchases made, or obstructions of different kinds offered, the complaint against which, even if the assembly of Meers at Hydurabad should be disposed to listen to such a complaint at all, must lead to long and irritating discussions, and yield little redress in the end. The perpetual residence of a British Agent, to take up the advocacy of such representations, will be indispensable, and his doing so, will produce continual bickering and discontent, and generate ill-will in those with whom he comes into collision. It is, however, most probable, that merchants will fear to incur the risk and trouble, incident to such adventures, and will thus allow the treaty to become a dead letter, like the commercial treaties already concluded with Siam and Cochin China, and even with the Burmese Court, where the British Government has a Resident Envoy to look after the execution of the stipulations entered into.

The East India Company in its earlier commercial treaties appears to have acted on a different principle, the extension of its own trade, and the privileges of its own boats, vessels, and merchandize, being the usual objects of stipulation and solicitude. Its agent was on the spot to conduct the trade, and to see that the conditions were not violated, and on this very footing, the Company had formerly a commercial treaty with Sindh, which soon after the establishment of the Talpoor Meers, was put an end to by the rude expulsion of the British Agent. The revival of negociation for a mere commercial treaty, with silence in respect to any Political object, appears calculated to produce an impression, that the Government still has a mercantile profit exclusively in view; and such an understanding will neither elevate its character, nor add to its weight and influence, in guiding the counsels of the different chiefs with whom relations of the kind may be established. But, after all, the great objection to such a connexion seems to be, that it offers no impediment to the courts with which we enter into such relations, opening or continuing intrigues and direct negociations with the very states against which it may be desired to make preparation. At the very time of entering upon the negociation with Sindh, it was known, that an agent from Persia was at Hydurabad, offering a daughter of the king in marriage to the favorite son of MEER MOORAD ULEE. If however the state of Sindh were allowed to connect itself in close relation with Persia, the commercial treaty we might conclude, would be no bar to the Russians insinuating themselves where the Persian court had paved the way for their influence. They might thus turn the resources of Sindh against us, or at least neutralize, or obstruct any advantage we might hope to derive from them, in the defence of the western frontier of India. If ever Hindoostan is invaded from the west, the battle must clearly be fought upon the Indus, and it would be a failure of common foresight, were measures not taken to secure, that the chiefs, states, and tribes, upon its banks, should be unanimous and hearty in their exertions to repel the invader. It may be said, however, that the time is not come for making provision for such objects: but whether the danger be near, or remote, it would scarcely be consistent with prudence to engage in measures likely to produce alienation, or to lower the respect and influence, which as holders in declared and full sovereignty of the principal part of Hindoostan, the British Government ought naturally to possess with the remainder.

Colonel POTTINGER, on receipt of his instructions, sent immediate intimation to the Meers of Sindh, and in particular to MEER MOORAD ULEE at Hydurabad, of his being commissioned by the Governor General to confer with them on some important matters, and he requested the requisite permission to proceed to Hydurabad for the purpose. This having been granted, after some demur, and the Bombay Government having provided the necessary escort, establishment, and equipment for the Envoy of the Supreme Government, Colonel POTTINGER moved from Kuchh, and arrived at Hydurabad in the course of February, 1832. He immediately explained the views of the British Government, and delivered the letter from the Governor General to MEER MOORAD ULEE, in which they were stated at length. A series of long and tedious discussions was then commenced, during which several projects and counter-projects, and drafts of treaties, were mutually exchanged. After much negociation, a Treaty was at last concluded with MEER MOORAD ULEE KHAN, on the part of the assembled Chiefs at Hydurabad, on the 20th April 1832, corresponding with which, the following Engagement was executed by the Governor General at Shimla on the 19th June following.

" A Treaty, consisting of seven Articles, having been " concluded on the 10th Zeehij 1247 A. H. corresponding " with 20th April 1832, between The Honorable East " India Company and His Highness MEER MOORAD " ALI KHAN Talpoor Buhadoor, Ruler of Hydurabad " in Sindh, through the Agency of Lieutenant-Colonel " HENRY POTTINGER, Envoy on the part of the British " Government, acting under the authority vested in him " by the Right Honorable Lord WILLIAM CAVENDISH " BENTINCK, G. C. B. and G. C. H., Governor General " of the British Possessions in India, this Engagement " has been given in writing at Shimla, this day, the 19th " June 1832, both in English and Persian, in token of " the perfect confirmation and acknowledgment of the " obligations which it contains, in the manner following:

Article I. " That the friendship provided for in for-" mer Treaties, between the British Government and " that of Sindh remain unimpaired and binding, and that " this stipulation has received additional efficacy through " the medium of Lieutenant-Colonel POTTINGER, Envoy, " &c. so that the firm connection and close alliance now " formed between the said States shall descend to the " Children and Successors of the House of the above " named MEER MOORAD ALI KHAN, principal after " principal, from generation to generation.

Article II. " That the two Contracting Powers bind " themselves never to look with the eye of covetousness " on the possessions of each other.

Article III. "That the British Government has "requested a passage for the merchants and traders of "Hindostan, by the river and roads of Sindh, by "which they may transport their goods and merchan-"dize from one country to another, and the said Govern-"ment of Hydurabad hereby acquiesces in the same "request on the three following conditions:

1st. "That no person shall bring any description of "Military Stores by the above river or roads.

2d. "That no armed vessels or boats shall come by the "said river.

3d. "That no English merchants shall be allowed to "settle in Sindh, but shall come as occasion "requires, and having stopped to transact their "business, shall return to India.

Article IV. "When merchants shall determine on "visiting Sindh, they shall obtain a passport to do so "from the British Government, and due intimation of "the granting of such passports shall be made to the "said Government of Hydurabad, by the Resident in "Kutch or other Officer of the said British Government.

Article V. "That the Government of Hydurabad "having fixed certain, proper, and moderate duties to "be levied on merchandize and goods proceeding by the "aforesaid routes, shall adhere to that scale, and not "arbitrarily and despotically either encrease or lessen "the same, so that the affairs of merchants and traders "may be carried on without stop or interruption, and "the custom-house officers and farmers of revenue "of the Sindh Government, are to be especially directed "to see that they do not delay the said merchants, on "pretence of awaiting for fresh orders from the Govern-"ment, or in the collection of the duties; and the said

" Government is to promulgate a Tariff, or table of " duties leviable on each kind of goods, as the case " may be."

Article VI. " That whatever portions of former " Treaties entered into between the two States which " have not been altered and modified by the present one, " remain firm and unaltered, as well as those stipulations " now concluded, and by the blessing of God, no devia- " tion from them shall ever happen."

Article VII. " That the friendly intercourse between " the two States shall be kept up by the dispatch of " Vakeels whenever the transaction of business, or the " encrease of the relations of friendship may render it " desirable."

The following Supplemental Engagement was also concluded with Meer Moorad Ulee Khan:—

" The following Articles of Engagement having been " agreed on, and settled on the 22d April, 1832, between " the Hon'ble East India Company and his Highness " MEER MOORAD ALI KHAN Talpoor Buhadoor, " Ruler of Hydurabad, in Sindh, as supplemental to the " Treaty concluded on the 20th April 1832, through the " Agency of Lieutenant Colonel HENRY POTTINGER, " Envoy on the part of the said Hon'ble East India " Company, under full power and authority vested in him " by the Right Hon'ble Lord WILLIAM CAVENDISH " BENTINCK, G. C. B. and G. C. H., Governor General " of the British Possessions in India: this Engagement " has been given in writing at Shimla, this day, the 19th " June 1832, both in English and Persian, in token of " the perfect confirmation and acknowledgment of the " obligations which it contains, in the manner following :

Article I. "It is inserted in the Vth Article of the "perpetual Treaty, that the Government of Hydurabad "will furnish the British Government with a statement "of duties, &c. and after that, the Officers of the British "Government, who are versed in affairs of traffic, "will examine the said statement. Should the state-"ment seem to them to be fair and equitable, and agreea-"ble to custom, it will be brought into operation, and "will be confirmed, but should it appear too high, His "Highness MEER MOORAD ALI KHAN, on hearing "from the British Government to this effect through "Colonel POTTINGER, will reduce the said duties.

Article II. "It is clear as noon-day, that the punish-"ment and suppression of the plunderers of Parkhur, the "Thull, &c. is not to be effected by any one Government, "and as this measure is incumbent on, and becoming the "States, as tending to secure the welfare and happiness "of their respective subjects and countries, it is hereby "stipulated, that on the commencement of the ensuing "rainy season, and of which MEER MOORAD ALI "KHAN shall give due notice, the British, Sindh, and "Jodhpoor Governments shall direct their joint and "simultaneous efforts to the above object.

Article III. "The Governments of the Honorable "East India Company and of Khyrpoor, namely, "MEER ROOSTUM, have provided in a treaty conclud-"ed between the States, that whatever may be settled "regarding the opening of the Indus at Hydurabad "shall be binding on the said contracting powers. It "is, therefore, necessary that copies of the Treaty should "be sent by the British and Hydurabad Governments "to MEER ROOSTUM KHAN for his satisfaction and "guidance."

CHAPTER ELEVENTH.

The character and policy of Runjeet Singh. His revenues. Strength of his army. General observations.

THE personal character of the present ruler of Lahôr and that of his government will best have been gathered, from the perusal of his acts, as related in the preceding Chapters; nevertheless it may be useful to sum up the result, and to explain the present condition of his territory, its resources, and the military means at this Chief's command.

It has before been stated, that RUNJEET SINGH had no education in any branch of learning or science. He cannot read or write in any language, but the habit of hearing papers read in Persian, Punjabee, and Hindee, and great assiduity in his attention, even to the minutiæ of business, have given him a facility in following, and understanding for the most part what is so submitted to him: so that, although quite unable to appreciate elegancies of style, or to dictate verbatim what should be written, he transacts business rapidly, is ready with a short and decided order upon any report or representation read to him, and when the draft of his instruction is submitted, after being prepared in due form, he sees at once whether it fully meets his view. Confidential secretaries are perpetually in attendance, and are frequently called up in the night, to expedite orders, as the sudden recollection, or caprice of the Muha-Raja, suggests the issuing of them. His memory is excellent, and stored with minute, as well as important circumstances. His disposition is at the same time watchful, and his eye quick and searching, so that nothing escapes his observation; while the perspicacity displayed in his appreciation of character, and in tracing the motives of other's actions, gives him a command and influence over all that approach him, which have been mainly instrumental to his rapid rise. With great acuteness, he has a lively imagination; and though never for an instant forgetful of any ends he may have in view, there is a frankness and naiveté about his conversation, peculiarly agreeable. His observations and remarks are given ordinarily in short, terse, incoherent phrase, or in the shape of interrogatories, but they are such, as remain fixed in the recollection of the person to whom they are addressed, as uncommon, and as displaying an original thinker. He has great power of dissimulation, and, under the greatest frankness of manner, and even familiarity in his intercourse, can veil subtle designs, and even treachery. In action he has always shown himself personally brave, and collected, but his plans betray no boldness or adventurous hazard. Address, and cunning, nay, even corruption, have always been preferred by him, as instruments of success, to any dash of enterprize, calculated to excite admiration or inspire awe. His fertility in expedients is wonderful, and he is never at a loss for a resource in the greatest difficulties, but many of his actions evince caprice, and even instability of purpose, for the motive of them cannot be traced or imagined. His uniform conduct and career through life, prove him to be selfish, sensual, and licentious in the extreme; disregardful of all ties of affection, blood, or friendship in the pursuit of ambition, or pleasure; and profligately greedy—plundering and reducing to misery without the slightest feeling, or remorse, widows, orphans and families possessing claims to consideration and respect, that one wonders should not have been recognized, even if it were only from policy. In his youth he was lavish in his gifts to favorites, and there was liberality in his general dealings, but, as age has come over him, avarice, and the desire of hoarding, have become the ruling passions, and he is approached, even by his confidential officers and those in favor, with more apprehension of robbery and exaction from themselves, than of hope to add to their accumulated means through his indulgence. His temper was in youth excellent, and always under command, but the irritability of an impaired constitution frequently now overpowers him, and he has been known to break out into fits of passion, and to descend to use personal violence towards the objects of his rage; but, withal, there is no ferocity in his disposition, and he has never taken life, even under circumstances of aggravated offence.

His stature is low, and the loss of an eye from the small pox takes away much from his appearance, which however is still far from being unprepossessing, for his countenance is full of expression and animation, and is set off with a handsome flowing beard, grey at 50 years of age, but tapering to a point below his breast. In his youth he must have had much vigour and activity, but he is now so emaciated, and weak, as to be compelled to adopt a singular method of mounting the tall horses, on which he loves to ride. A man kneels down before him, and he throws his leg over his neck, when the man rises with the Muha-Raja mounted on his shoulders: he then approaches the horse, and RUNJEET SINGH, putting his right foot into the stirrup, and holding by the mane, throws his left over the man's head, and the back of the horse, into the stirrup on the other side. His love of his horses is extreme, and has been already several times mentioned. He has them continually in his sight, covered with jewels and rich caparisons, and they are the objects of his frequent caresses. He is himself plain and simple in dress, and quite unreserved in all his habits; and his diet consists of high stimulants of which he partakes sparingly. He has great delight however in military parade, and display, and spends nearly the half of every day in seeing reviews, or examining equipments, or in some way studying to promote the efficiency of some branch of his army. He also seems to take pleasure in seeing his courtiers and establishments decorated in jewels and handsome dresses, and it is not to be denied, that they show considerable taste, for the splendour of the display of his Durbar is very striking. Although no bigot, and active in restraining the zeal and fanaticism of the Akalees, and others, RUNJEET SINGH is yet scrupulous in the performance of all the prescribed observances of the Sikh faith, and, for a certain number of hours every day, has the Grunth read before him by Gooroos, and is liberal in his charities to Fuqeers and men of reputed sanctity. He is indeed superstitious in the extreme, readily conceiving fancies in respect to his destiny, and fortunes, and never failing to consult astrologers before entering upon any important undertaking.

With respect to the policy and internal Government of RUNJEET SINGH, the most remarkable feature is, the entire absence of any thing like system, or principle in his management. His career throughout has been that of an encroaching usurper, and seizer of all within his reach, but what he has so possessed himself of, he subjects to no systematic administration. The whole is committed to farmers, with full power to deal with the lives and properties of the producing classes of the population, RUNJEET SINGH trusting to his own military means, for the control of these farmers, and for the exaction from them of any extra gains he may learn that they have made. Nevertheless his extortions are directed chiefly against the old Sikh families, and his own state officers: merchants and traders are protected, and the duties and taxes, to which they are subjected, are not for the most part immoderate. RUNJEET SINGH has however shown a disposition himself to become a dealer in some articles, as in shawls, salt, &c. and all that he touches becomes of course monopoly, or in some other shape the source of exaction and corrupt gain.

It cannot be said, that RUNJEET SINGH has yet given to the Punjab any constitution or fixed form of Government. There is no law, written or oral, and no courts of justice have been any where established. The Gooroo-Mata, or old council of the Sikhs, has, with every other institution adapted to the state of things which existed before the establishment of the supremacy of the present ruler, been entirely discontinued. The last council of the kind was held, when Holkur fled into the Punjab, and the British armies followed in pursuit, and it was a question what part the Sikhs as a nation should take in the juncture. RUNJEET SINGH, though the most influential chief, pretended not then to any supremacy of dominion, and the question was one, which, as it concerned the whole body of the Sikhs, required that all should have a voice in determining. At present the Government appears to be a pure despotism, the standing army, ever ready for active service, and eager to be employed where plunder and exaction are the objects, forms the whole machinery of administration. By it only the treasury is filled, and control exercised over state officers, powerful subjects, and indeed over every class of the population. The personal influence, and verbal orders of the head of the state, form again the exclusive hold upon the discipline and affections of the troops. Thus the whole power and authority centres in the single individual, whom fortune, and his own abilities have placed at the head of affairs; and, upon his being removed from the scene, unless there be another to fill his place, with equal energy, and command over the attachment and affections of his dependents, which, it is to be feared, is not the character of KHURUK SINGH, every thing must necessarily fall into confusion.

The territorial possessions of RUNJEET SINGH, comprize now the entire fork of the Punjab, as bounded by the Indus and Sutlej, the two extreme rivers. He holds besides Kashmeer, and the entire hill country to the snowy range, and even Ludak beyond the Heemalaya: for though many of the Rajas of this tract still remain in their possessions, they have been reduced to the character of subjects, paying tribute equal to their utmost means, and contributing men to the armies of Lahôr, whenever called upon. Besides this extensive territory, RUNJEET SINGH has abont 45 Talooks entire, or in share with others, on the British side of the Sutlej; and westward of the Indus, he holds Khyrabad, Akona, and Peshawur, Durra-Ghazee-Khan, which has been farmed to the Nuwab of Buhawulpoor, and Durra-Ismaeel-Khan, assigned to HAFIZ AHMED KHAN of Munkera, as before related. He also levies tributes from the Balooch Chiefs of Tonk and Sâgur to the southward. Captain MURRAY estimates that the amonnt of Land Revenue and Tributes, annually levied from the whole of these possessions, is .... *Rupees.* 1,24,03,900

Besides which, the Customs of the Punjab yield to RUNJEET SINGH, ... 19,00,600

An Item, called Mohurana, being a Fee on every paper submitted for the Seal of RUNJEET SINGH, ... 5,77,000

Making a total Khalsa Revenue of 1,48,81,500

The same Officer estimates that there remains, still appropriated in Jageers, or held by old Sikh families, and establishments, without paying any thing to the Khalsa, territory yielding, ... 1,09,28,000

Thus making the entire resources of the country under the dominion of RUNJEET, Rs. 2,58,09,500

This total is not very wide of the revenue set down in the books of the Moghul Government, as the produce of the Lahôr Sooba; and, considering that Kashmeer, and some territory south of the Sutlej is included, the correspondence of amount is in favor of the correctness of the estimate, for the province cannot be so productive under the Sikhs, as it was in the peaceable times of the Moghul dominion.

RUNJEET SINGH has for many years been hoarding treasure, and the fort of Govindgurh, built by him, and kept always in excellent repair, is the principal place for its deposit. Captain MURRAY, speaking from the best information he could collect, which, however, was necessarily very imperfect, and vague, estimates the value of the property accumulated by RUNJEET SINGH in cash, jewels, horses, and elephants, to be not less than ten crores of rupees, or the same number of millions of pounds sterling. By some the estimate is carried much higher, but such computations, being for the most part conjectural, err generally on the side of excess.

The military force of the Lahôr State is set down by the same officer, and his authority is the safest to follow on the point, as follows:

	Men.
1st. The available regular troops, Cavalry disciplined by Monsieur ALLARD, and the special troops mounted on horses of the State, the Gorchur, and Gorchur Khas, ...	12,811
Infantry, Disciplined Battalions, Nujeebs, and troops, more or less drilled under the eye of the Muha-Raja,..	14,941

Total regular troops, horse and foot,		27,752
Garrison corps, including the troops employed in Kashmeer,—Cavalry, ...	3000	
Infantry, variously armed and equipped,........................	23,950	26,950
Contingents of Sirdars, consisting, in the plains, principally of cavalry, but in the hills of foot soldiers,......		27,312
Total troops, horse and foot, ...		82,014

The artillery of RUNJEET SINGH consists of 376 guns, and 370 swivels, mounted on the backs of camels, or on light carriages adapted to their size. For these, there is no corps of artillery regimented, and organized, as is the custom in European armies, but there is a Darogha, at the head of a large establishment, which if RUNJEET SINGH were making preparation for a siege, could not be set down at less than 4 or 5000 men; but in time of peace, or when no such operation was in agitation, the number would be infinitely reduced. Several of the corps of cavalry, and all the battalions of infantry, have guns attached to them, the gunners of which are borne on the strength of the respective corps. The *Jinsee*, or heavy train only, is distinct from the rest of the army.

The above accumulation of resources, and of force, has grown up, and been produced entirely by the care and exertions of the Muha-Raja. His father left him nothing, but a body of Sikh cavalry, little superior to that of his neighbours, who have all now been reduced to the condition of subjects. RUNJEET SINGH has, in the formation especially of his military force, evinced the same enquiring activity, the same attention to minutiæ, and perseverance in watching the execution of his plans, which characterized the first Peter of Russia; and, compared with all that we see and hear of other chiefs who have raised themselves to high dominion, he ranks amongst those, whose means have been the least exceptionable, his career being stained by no bloody executions, and by much fewer crimes, than are chargeable against most founders of dynasties. The want of a generalizing mind, to refer things to fixed principles, and to lead to the formation or adoption of systems, and a deficiency of the intelligence resulting from education, or from habitual converse with men of high cultivation, have been the main defects of his character, and are the causes of RUNJEET SINGH'S Government being based on no solid forms, and institutions, which can be reckoned upon to carry on the machine, when the present regulator of all is removed from the scene. But where were such to be found amongst an association of Sikh banditti, formed from the outcasts of society, and from the dregs in particular of the agricultural class, men all in most desperate circumstances and driven by want to adopt the life of robbers? All that was educated, and refined, had disappeared from the Punjab, before RUNJEET SINGH was born. The natural effect however of the union of authority in his person, has been, to create a court, where, in the course of time, science and refinement will be reproduced, or collected from the countries around, as the habits of peace and luxury, come to supercede the bustle, and perpetual activity of war and military expeditions.

And let not those, who are disposed to give to RUNJEET SINGH the credit due to him as founder of a kingdom and dynasty, take exception at the circumscribed limit of his dominion, as lowering his merit in comparison with others, The circumstances of his position, with the British Government on one side,—fresh risen to a majesty of power, that it would have been madness for him to think of encountering, and with the prejudiced and fanatic Moosulman population of Afghanistan upon every other frontier, have been barriers against extension, which it was impossible to overcome, and effectually forbad the hope of carrying the Sikh dominion beyond its present limits. The gain that has already been made upon the latter, and the manner in which the brave and bigotted Mohummedans, have, in many instances, been reconciled to the sway of a hated, and even despised sect, are amongst the most creditable features of the policy, and career of RUNJEET SINGH.

Towards the British Government his conduct has been marked with equal sagacity. Careful not to offend to the point leading to actual rupture, he contrived to make his gain of the juncture, at the very moment when the British Government stept forward to confine his dominion to the Sutlej, and to wrest from his grasp, the valuable tract between that river and the Jumna, which was all held by Sikhs, and regarded by him therefore as his legitimate and certain prey. When the ill-will and suspicion, engendered by this interference, had subsided, and he felt assured that the interposing Government had no desire to push its conquests, or further to interfere with his ambitious views, he cultivated the friendship of its officers, and has since desired to exhibit himself to the world as united by close relations, and on the best understanding with it. He seems to be now thoroughly convinced, that its friendship, and engagements may be relied upon, and there cannot be a doubt, that if ever the occasion should arise, to render it necessary to make preparation against invasion from the west, he would side heartily with us, and show zeal in repelling the invader. His professions, his interest, and his inclinations, are all for us at present, and he derives no little strength and security, from giving it out, that he is on such terms with the British nation.

Having thus conducted the reader, in the foregoing pages, through the gradations by which the Sikh power has been raised to its present flourishing and imposing condition, it remains to lay before him some insight into the habits and manners peculiar to this sect, to enable him to appreciate the character of the nation, and the peculiar traits which distinguish it from the rest of the population of Hindoostan. This has been amply done to hand by Captain MURRAY, who has collected, in an Appendix to the report he laid before Lord WILLIAM BENTINCK, the result of his own observations, during a residence of more than fifteen years amongst the Sikhs, attended with hourly intercourse with individuals of all classes, added to the necessity of listening, to representations of all descriptions, with a view to the arbitration or adjustment of their disputes. Captain MURRAY'S remarks and the facts he has collected, though put together without much regard to arrangement, and evidently with no view to publication, are nevertheless so replete with useful information and intelligence, that to withhold them would be unpardonable. On the other hand, the weight of the authority would be lost if they were to be recast and combined into a more studied form by another hand. It is proposed, therefore, to conclude this little volume, by the transfer verbatim into it of the Appendix, devoted by this officer to the delineation of "the Manners, Rules, and Customs of the Sikhs." The curious reader will be well repaid the labour of a perusal.

APPENDIX.

ON THE MANNERS, RULES, AND CUSTOMS OF THE SIKHS,

BY CAPTAIN W. MURRAY.

THE accomplishments of reading and writing are uncommon amongst the Sikhs, and are chiefly confined to Hindoo and Moosulman *Mootsuddees*, or clerks, who acquire a sufficient knowledge of the Persian language, to enable them to keep the accounts, and to conduct the epistolary correspondence of the Chiefs. The *Goormookha*, or Punjabee written dialect, is familiar to many Sikhs; but, in general, they express a rooted aversion to the acquisition of the Arabic and Persian languages, resulting chiefly from the ideas instilled, and prejudices imbibed in early age against every thing, however useful and rational, that bears relation to, and is connected with, the religion and education of the Moosulmans.

Concerns are transacted by oral testimony, verbal agreements, and promises. The test of right is confined to the memory of the oldest inhabitants of a neighbourhood, and tradition preserves old customs. Falsehood, fraud, and perjury are the natural concomitants of such a mode of conducting affairs. Money, fear, and favor, can purchase an oath, can determine a village boundary dispute, and screen a criminal from detection, and the infliction of punishment. In some instances an accused person will call for the *Dibb*, or ordeal of innocence, plunge his fingers in boiling oil, bear a heated ploughshare on his hands for 50 to 100 yards, challenge his accuser to the trial by water, and, if he escape unhurt, his purity is declared, and freely acknowledged.

Witchcraft and spells, (*Jadoo* and *Moot*), have a powerful influence over the fancies and actions of the Chiefs and other inhabitants of the Sikh States. A sudden indisposition, a vomiting of blood, or any unusual ailment, for the nature and cause of which a native cannot very readily account, are generally attributed to the malice and invention of a rival, or to an evil disposed member of the family. The possession of a waxen or dough effigy, some party-colored threads, and small human bones discovered in the dwelling, or about the person of a suspected individual, are convincing proofs of guilt and wickedness.*

* "The harmless flame, which insensibly," says GIBBON, "melted a waxen image, might derive a powerful and pernicious energy from the affrighted fancy of the person whom it was maliciously designed to represent." One of the reasons RAJA JUSWUNT SINGH of Nabah, assigned for his wish to disinherit his eldest son and heir was, that he had been engaged in some mischievous practises, and destructive enchantments, with one BHAEE DIGHANOO, to ruin the health of his father. Sirdar BHOOP SINGH of Roopur, advanced a similar charge against his uncle DARWA SINGH. Both these Chiefs bear the character of being well informed men, and wiser than their neighbours. RUTUN KOONWUR, the widow of MUHTAB SINGH, Chief of Thanesur, adopted a sickly boy, to whom she became immoderately attached, and vainly hoped he might be

Good and bad omens,* lucky and unlucky days, and particular hours of the day and night for commencing a journey and returning home, are carefully observed by the Sikhs, and by all other classes in the Punjab, whether engaged in the most momentous enterprizes, or in the common concerns of life. Prior to the field being taken with an army,† a visit of ceremony being paid to a distant friend, or a pilgrimage being made, the Muhoorut, or auspicious moment for departure, and return, must be

admitted to succeed to the landed property she held for life. In 1828, the boy died, and RUTTUN KOONWUR, in a paroxism of grief, filed a formal complaint, charging his death, through magical arts, to her nephew JUMERUT SINGH, producing in Court some body clothes, and on no better evidence directing her Vakeel to prosecute him for murder. The case was set at rest by reasoning on its absurdity, and RUTUN KOONWUR consoled herself by the adoption of another boy. In September 1829, a Thanadar of the Thanesur Ranee, hanged a Brahmin suspected of magic. The Ranee dismissed the Thanadar from his situation.

* To hear a partridge call on your right hand as you enter a town—cranes passing from left to right—meeting a bareheaded person—a jackass braying as you enter a town or village—a dog shaking his head and ears on quitting home—to meet a corpse or a Brahmin—to hear a female jackall howling during the night—sneezing on going out or coming into a house or room, &c. &c. are bad omens. The contrary are good omens. To hear a partridge call on your left—cranes passing from right to left—to meet a Mehtur or Sweeper—to behold pearls in your sleep. If a Moosulman dream of seeing the moon, it is as good as an *interview with the Prophet, &c. &c.*—An eminent Native Merchant came to me on business from Umritsur, and died at Loodeeana, of the Cholera Morbus. His followers very gravely told me that my remedies must be unavailing, for on entering the town, many bare-headed men of the Goojur cast had been met by the deceased.

† A gang of burglars being brought before me in 1819, admitted in evidence, that two pieces of coloured muslin had been tossed over their left shoulders, on hearing a jackall call on their right hand, soon after quitting Kurnal, where the burglary had been perpetrated. Dessa-Sool, or unlucky days—Saturday and Monday, to the east—Sunday and Friday, to the west—Tuesday and Wednesday, to the north, and Thursday to the south. The contrary are Siddh Jôg, or lucky days.

predicted by a Pundit, and the Pundit on his part is guided by the *jogme* or spirits; which pervade every quarter of the compass. To avert the pernicious consequences likely to ensue from unfavorable prognostics or dreams, charity is recommended, and in general given very freely on such occasions, by natives of rank and wealth. These, and many hundred other absurd prejudices and superstitious notions, are carried into the most solemn affairs of state. It is no uncommon practise of RUNJEET SINGH, when he contemplates any serious undertaking, to direct two slips of paper to be placed on the *Grunth Sohil*, or sacred volume of the Sikhs. On the one is written his wish, and on the other the reverse. A little boy is then brought in, and told to bring one of the slips, and, whichever it may happen to be, his Highness is as satisfied as if it were a voice from heaven. A knowledge of these whims, and prepossessions, is useful and necessary. They obtain, under varied shapes, and in diversified shades, throughout the Eastern world, warping the opinions, and directing the public and private affairs of all ranks in society, from he despot to the peasant, from the soldier in the battle-field, to the criminal at the tree of execution. It must be a pleasing duty to every public servant to endeavour to gain the confidence, and win the affections of the Chiefs and people

* When the Surhind Division, composed entirely of Sipahees, was directed, under the command of SIR DAVID OCHTERLONY, against the Goorkha power in 1814, it was suggested by NUND SINGH, the accredited agent of RUNJEET SINGH, that the first march should be made at the Dusehra. It being mentioned to him, that this was too early, he begged that the tents and a few men might move out on that day. He was gratified, and the success that attended this Division in all its operations, was attributed more to the choice of an auspicious hour, than to the wisdom, prudence, and gallantry of its commander, his officers, and men.

of a conquered country, by the impression of his acquaintance with, and seeming regard to their peculiarities and propensities, and in the superintendence and management of their concerns, to know the bents by which he may seize and work upon them. To touch upon such feelings without giving offence, demands on all occasions, the exercise of discretion, temper, and judgment: but when successfully done, it is easy by a kindly manner and persuasive address, to lead the misguided and ignorant from error and antiquated usages, to appreciate the advantages attendant on intellectual improvement, and the benefits resulting from science and moral feeling.

In the Sikh States, the administration of civil and criminal justice is vested in the Sirdar, or chief. Crimes and trespasses, as in the middle ages, are atoned for by money: the fines are unlimited by any rule, and generally levied arbitrarily according to the means of the offender, whose property is attached, and his family placed under restraint to enforce payment. These amerciaments form a branch of revenue to the chief, and a fruitful source of peculation to his officers, who too frequently have recourse to the most harsh and cruel means to elicit confessions, and extort money for real or imaginary offences. He who gains his point, pays his *Shookurana*, or present of gratitude, and he who is cast, pays his *Jureemana*, or penalty. The wealthy may secure justice, but the indigent are likely to obtain something less. The larger the bribe the more chance of success. A case where the right is clear and undeniable, is often allowed to lie over, that the present may be augmented. All officers under the chief, and employed by him in districts and departments, follow his example; but are ultimately thrown into a *bora*, or dungeon, and required to refund, and when they have satisfied the cupidity of their superior, they are generally permitted to resume their functions, honored with the shawl as a mark of favor. Capital punishment is very seldom inflicted. The most incorrigible culprits are punished with the loss of either one or both hands, and deprivation of nose or ears; but mutilation is rare, for whoever has the means to pay, or can procure a respectable security to pay for him within a given time, may expiate the most heinous transgressions*.

On the commission of a *daka* or burglary, a *quzzakee*†, or highway robbery, the chief, within whose jurisdiction the act has been perpetrated, is called upon to make restitution; and, should he decline, the chief whose subject has suffered, resorts to the *Lex talionis*, and drives off several hundred head of cattle, or retaliates in some way or other. This summary method of obtaining indemnification for all robberies attended with aggravating circumstances, is a measure of absolute necessity, as many of the petty Chiefs, their Officers and Zumeendars, harbour thieves, and participate in their guilty practises.

When a petty theft is substantiated, either through the medium of a *Muhur-khaee*, or the production of a *Mooddo* or *Numoona*, (the confession of one of the thieves, or a part of the stolen property) the sufferer has generally,

* Statutes were passed in the reigns of HENRY 8th, EDWARD 6th, ELIZABETH, and JAMES 1st, sanctioning, and directing the loss of the right and left hand, and of an ear, for offences which would by a Sikh, scarcely be deemed deserving the infliction of a mulct.

† This is an Arabic or Turkish word. In the provincial dialect we have Dharwee.

as a preliminary to pay the *Chuharum*, or fourth, as a perquisite to the Chief, or his Thanadar, ere he can recover the amount of his losses. Independent of this, the *Muhur-khaes*, or approver, generally stipulates for a full pardon, and that no demand shall be made on the confessing delinquent for his *Kundee*, viz. any, or such portion of the property, as may have accrued to him as his dividend of the spoil. This share of the spoil becomes chargeable to the other thieves, and on settling accounts it is distributed equally amongst them.

In all cases of stolen cattle, it is an established rule when the *Soorāgh-Khoj*, or trace of the footsteps, is carried to the gate, or into the fields of any village, the Zumeendars of that village must either shew the track beyond their own boundary, and allow the village to be searched, or pay the value of the cattle.*

The rules of succession to landed property in the Sikh States are arbitrary, and are variously modified in accordance to the usages, the interests and prejudices of different families, nor is it practicable to reduce the anomalous system to a fixed and leading principle. A distinction obtains in the Canons of Inheritance, between the Manjhee and Malwa Sikhs, or Singhs: the former are so termed from the tract situated between the Ravee and Beeah rivers, from which they originally sprung, migrating thence and extending their conquests through the Punjab, and into the Sirhind province, where being of a military and predatory character, they soon conquered

* Hume, in treating of the Anglo-Saxons, says "If any man could track his stolen cattle into another's ground, the latter was obliged to shew the tracks out of it, or pay their value."

for themselves a permanent possession. The Malwa Chiefs, are the Puteeala, Jheend, and Naba Rajahs, and the Bhaee of Khytul. The three first named are descendants of a common ancestor named PHOOL, who was Choudhuree of a village near Balenda, and are from him often collectively styled the Phoolkeean. The progenitor of the Bhaee of Khytul, having rendered some service to one of the Sikh Gooroos, the appellation of Bhaee, or brother, was conferred upon him as a mark of distinguished approbation; and the persons of all the Bhaees are consequently held in a degree of respect above their fellows.

The practice of succession to property, both real and personal, amongst the Manjhee Singhs, is by *Bhaee-bund* and *Choonda-bund*. The first being an equal distribution of all lands, forts, tenements, and moveables, among sons, with, in some instances, an extra or double share to the eldest termed "*Khurch-Sirdaree*," assimilating to the double share in the law of Moses.* Choonda-bund is an equal division among mothers for their respective male issue.†

When a Manjhee Singh dies, leaving no male offspring, his brothers, or his nephews of the full blood, assume the right of succession, to which the widow or widows become competitors. According to the Shasters, (if they

* Deuteronomy, Chap. xxi, v. 15, 16, 17.

† This practice of Choonda-bund is agreeable to the Hindoo Law. VYARA says "If there be many sons of one man, by different mothers, but in equal number and alike by class, a distribution amongst the mothers is approved to Brihaspati." If there be many springs from one, alike in number and in class, but born of rival mothers, partition must be made by them, according to law, by the allotment of shares to the mothers.

may be considered applicable to public property and Chiefships,) the prior title of the widows is held ;* but the Sikhs, with a view to avoid an open and direct violation of a known law, have a custom termed *Kurawa* or *Chadur-dula*, which obtains in every family, with the exception to those of the Bhaees. The eldest surviving brother of the deceased places a white robe over, and the *neeth*, or ring in the nose of the widow, which ceremony constitutes her his wife.

This practice accords with the Hindoo and Mosaic Laws† and acts as a counteractive to the many evils attendant on female rule. If the free will of the widow were consulted, it is scarcely to be doubted, she would prefer the possession of power, and the charms of liberty, to the alternative of sacrificing her claims to her brother-in-law, and taking her station amongst his rival wives. Judging from the masculine disposition,—want of modesty, and of delicate feeling, which form the characteristic feature of Sikh females, necessity, and not choice, must have led them to yield to the adoption of an usage, which must often be repugnant to their natures, and disgusting to their thoughts.

On failure of brothers and nephews, the general practice is, equal division of lands, and personal effects, amongst the surviving widows of Manjhee Singhs.

* In the Bengal and most generally current Shasters, this is the rule: but not in the Mithila province, (Tirhoot, &c.) the widow is there excluded, and receives only a maintenance.

† Deuteronomy, Chap. xxv, v. 5 to 10.

† Yajuyawoleya says, "If a brother die without male issue, let another approach the widow once in the proper season." And Menu ordains, "having espoused her in due form, she being clad in a white robe."

Adoption by the widows is not allowed, and the female line is entirely excluded from the succession, to prevent the estates merging in the possessions of another family.

The inconvenience, and evil, originating in the prevailing practice amongst the Manjhee families, of successive and minute sub-divisions of landed property, aggravated by the system of coparcenary possession, are seen, felt, and acknowledged, and the mischief of such a system cannot be too soon remedied.*

Amongst the Malwa Singhs, the rights of primogeniture in the males are respected, and Jageers, or grants of land, are assigned for the maintenance of younger sons, by which the many inconveniences, noticed in the practice, or rule established amongst the Manjhee families, are obviated.

* The Agrarian Law thus adopted amongst the Manjhee Singhs, and the condition to which it has reduced many families, may receive illustration from the analogous picture drawn by Sir John Davis in his work entitled *Discovery of the causes, why Ireland was never entirely subdued by the English.* " The custom of Gavil-kind did breed another mischief, for " thereby every man being born to land, as well bastard, as legitimate, " they all held themselves to be gentlemen. And though their portions " were never so small, and themselves never so poor, for Gavil-kind must " needs in the end make a poor gentility, yet did they scarce descend to " husbandry, or merchandize, or to learn any mechanical art or science. " Besides these poor gentlemen were so affected to their small portions of " land, that they rather chose to live at home by theft, extortions and " cashering than to seek any better fortunes abroad. The lesser proprietors " should be encouraged to attach themselves to, and acknowledge the " authority of some neighbouring superior. This is an arrangement that " will not be attended with the least loss to them in a pecuniary point of " view, and it will ensure the certainty of having so many horse at command under one leader, instead of having many individuals, without a " head, or what is worse, so insignificant, as not to be remembered in a " moment of exigency."

The Malwa Singhs, with exception to the Bhaees, sanction and admit the usage of *Kurawa*, thereby opposing a bar to disputed succession between the brothers, nephews, and the widows of a deceased chief.

The Bhaees of Khytul, and other places, although they reject the union by *Kurawa*, yet set aside the claims of a widow, in favor of the brothers and nephews of one dying without male issue. The widows of Bhaees receive small Jageers for their support during life.

The Mahomedan families scattered over the Sikh States, who have been enabled to preserve their existence, and the shadow of power, reject the ordinances of their Law-givers, and are guided by rules of their own forming. Were the Mahomedan and Hindoo laws on inheritance, as inculcated by the *Shura* and *Metakshara*, to be made the leading principle in succession to landed property, very few, if any, of the many principalities in India would remain entire, and a common distribution would become universal, to the extinction of great estates, and the annihilation of the chiefs with their aristocratical influence.

When the country, overrun by the Sikhs, had been parcelled out into new allotments, the former divisions into districts, as established during the reigns of the Dehlee Emperors, and recorded by the *Kanoongoes*, or rule-tellers, became void, and much angry litigation arose in respect to the village boundaries, and waste lands. The cultivators originated the cause of dispute, and the effect was in most cases an appeal to arms, and an effusion of blood, before the claims of the parties could be heard, and decided by a convention of neighbouring Zumeendars, selected to draw a line of demarcation, and bound by a solemn oath to act impartially.* The litigants made choice of an equal number of *Moonsifs* or arbitrators, in some cases one each, in others two to three each. These committees would prolong their sittings for weeks and months, being all the while fed and paid by the parties, caressed and threatened by their chiefs, their relatives and friends, influenced by party spirit, governed by fear, and little verifying the saying common amongst them of "*Punch men Purmêsur.*" Five different modes of accommodation were in general adoption amongst these Punchayts—1st, An equal division of the land in dispute.—2nd, The Punchayt selected the oldest and most respectable member of their committee to define the limit, the others consenting to abide by his award.—3rd, A moiety of the line of demarcation was drawn by the arbiters of the one party, and the remaining portion by those of the other.—4th, The Punchayt referred the final adjustment to an old inhabitant of a neighbouring village, upon whose local knowledge and experience they placed more reliance than on their own limited information.—5th, It sometimes occurred to the Punchayt to leave the division in the hands of one of the disputants, whose probity and reputation were established in the vicinity.

Village boundary disputes, attended with aggravating circumstances, between the Chiefs and cultivators of

* The oath administered to the person who erects the boundary pillars, if a Hindoo, is the Gunga-Jul, or the Chour, or raw hide of the cow, or swearing by his son. If a Moossulman, the Qoran, or the placing his hands on his son's head. The Chour, and sweafing by his own child, are the most binding.

contiguous and rival states, are of daily occurrence, and the right and title to the smallest slip of land is contested with an obstinacy quite disproportionate to its intrinsic value. Little attention is paid by the Chiefs or their subjects to the justice or reasonableness of a case; it is quite sufficient, according to Sikh notions, that a claim be advanced and presented, as something may be obtained, and nothing can be lost by the reference to a Punchayt, which will use its endeavours to please, and harmonize its decision to the wants and wishes of those by whom it has been selected.

Bloodshed between Zumeendars in a boundary dispute, is sometimes atoned for by giving a *nata*, or daughter, in marriage to a relative of the deceased, or commuted to the payment of 150 to 200 rupees, or 125 beegahs of land. In general, however, revenge is sought, and the *Khoon-buha*, or price of blood, deemed insufficient satisfaction, particularly when a mother has to lament the loss of a favorite child, or a wife with a family, the bereavement of a husband.

Claims to islands in a river flowing between two Manors, and to alluvions, are determined by what is called the *Kuchmuch*, or *Kishtee-bunna*, which practice or rule assigns the land to the proprietor of the bank, or main, upon which the alluvion is thrown, and from which the water has receded. If the island be formed in the centre of the river, and there be depth of water on each side of it, sufficient for boats to ply, in this case it becomes the joint property of the Chiefs on both banks.*

* This appears a very ancient custom, being mentioned by BLACKSTONE, who derives his information from *Bracton*.

This custom which obtains in the Sikh States, with regard to alluvion, is universal, so far as my knowledge in the local laws and usages of India has extended, wherever lands are liable to such accident by an alteration in the course of rivers. In the case of lands cast by the change of the stream from one side of the river to the other, though one Chief gains, and another loses, yet it is customary to preserve the rights of the Zemindar, if he consent to cultivate the lands. The decided enmity of two Chiefs is seldom a bar to an arrangement, in which each finds or perceives an advantage to himself, either immediate or prospective, for streams in India are so subject to change, that the land lost one rainy season may be regained in the next, or èven in the cold weather, when the river falls and the floods cease.

The use and abuse of the ancient privilege of the Zumeendars in damming up, and turning the course of a stream into artificial *Kools*, or cuts, for the purpose of irrigating the lands in its vicinity, causes disputes and bloodshed ; and, after much angry dissention, the result is generally a compromise stipulating for a reciprocal enjoyment of the gifts of nature. In some instances, and in contiguous estates, the parties will agree to take equal shares of the water, either by the hour, or the day, or by measurement; in other cases, one will receive two-thirds, and his neighbour one-third only, according to their respective and pressing wants. The land-holders, whose possessions are adjacent to the hills from which and their base, these streams and springs take their rise, require and demand a very large portion of the water for their rice lands, into which it is diverted by numberless water-courses, drawn with great ingenuity by the cultivators into distant and countless parterres. Those who hold land at a distance, and lower down the river, in the more arid districts, are querulous, that the streams do not flow unobstructed in their natural course, which would give them the unabsorbed portion to irrigate their wheat and barley crops.

It seems to be a question how far a Chief may be justified in entirely obstructing the course of a natural stream, and in appropriating the waters to his own exclusive advantage, to the serious detriment and loss of his neighbours, whose rights he may seem bound to respect, so far as they have relation to property. On the whole, it appears most just, that all should partake, as far as circumstances will admit, of a share in the water of a natural stream or rivulet, and that when the absolute wants of those on the upper part of the stream have been supplied, the surplus should be again turned into, and permitted to flow in its bed, to satisfy others lower down, whether for irrigation, or the consumption of the people, and cattle, in the arid districts. The lesser currents do not swell in the hot months, as is the case with the larger rivers, which debouche from the Himala, and are fed in warm weather by the liquefaction of the snow: the supply of water in them is hence often so scanty, as scarcely to administer to the necessities of those near their heads, whilst the distress of others, farther down the stream, induces them to become more clamourous as the quantity decreases, and ultimately stops short of them.

Bunds, or dams, are always constructed, after the ains have ceased, to raise the water to a level with the surface, and to render it applicable to the purposes of irrigation; were a total prohibition of this beneficial practice to be enacted, large tracts on many estates, through which streams flow, in deep channels, would become uncultivated; and the villages depopulated, to the serious loss of the proprietors, and the ruin of their Zumeendars. With the view of relieving the deficiencies experienced from the want of the fluid in the arid districts lower down, a substitute for the dam might be found in a Hydraulic wheel of simple construction, to draw the water to the level, and in places where the banks are comparatively low, it will only be requisite to dig the *kool*, or cut, for the reception and carriage of the water deeper, and to raise it in the cut by sluice boards. The *churras*, or leathern bags, in common use at wells, with a relief of bullocks, might also be serviceable in other spots. All these expedients, however, fall very short of the utility and cheapness of the dams, when water requires to be conveyed many miles, and every *kool* is a canal in miniature.

Nuptial contracts are made in early youth by the parents or nearest of kin, who, in too many cases, are influenced more by pecuniary and sordid motives, than by the welfare of the children. Disagreements are very common relative to betrothments, (*mungnee*), and to breaches of a promise of marriage, (*nata* or *nisbut*) amongst all classes of the inhabitants. In some instances, real or imaginary diseases, or bodily defects, will be alleged by one of the contracting parties, as a reason why the bargain should be annulled; in others, a flaw in the cast, and in most a discovery, that the girl had been promised to two, three, or four different families, from all of which the needy parents or guardians had received money, ornaments, or clothes. If both parties be the subjects of one Chief, they appear before him, and either he, or his officers, satisfies them, or refers the decision to a Punchayt of the same class as the disputants. If tho complainant and defendant happen to reside in separate jurisdictions, and either of the Chiefs persevere in evading a compliance with the rule in such cases, or reject the award of a Punchayt, *Gaha,* or self-indemnification, is adopted by the opposite party, and the subjects, property, and cattle of his neighbour are picked up, and detained until satisfaction be offered and procured. The other side issues its letters of marque, and this pernicious system is frequently carried to the commission of serious outrage, and to infractions of the public tranquillity.*

It is not a rare occurrence for a parent or a guardian to be convicted of marrying a girl to one man, after her betrothment to another. The Chief, or a Punchayt, in general, in such cases, gives a verdict that the plaintiff is entitled to a female from the family; and if there be not one, the parents or guardian must find a substitute; or, as a *dernier* expedient, to which the injured party very unwillingly assents, the money he may have expended, or a trifle in excess with interest, is decreed to be restored to him, that he may find a spouse elsewhere.

* A demand was made on the state of Putteeala, by a subject of the Nabah Rajah, for the price of a buffaloe valued at 15 Rupees, but which on the settlement of the account by reprisal, exceeded 900. The case is still in dependance between them. Between the same states and by the same system, one rupee accumulated in a few years to 1500.

Amongst all the Jât families,† and some others of the lower classes in the Punjab, a custom prevails, on the demise of one brother leaving a widow, for a surviving brother to take his sister-in-law to wife by *Kurawah or Chadurdalna,* (see inheritance.) The offspring by the connexion are legitimate, and entitled to succeed to a share of all the landed and personal property.‡ It is optional with the widow, to take, either the eldest, (Jeth), or the youngest, who is generally preferred and deemed most suitable. Should she determine to relinquish worldly ideas, and to reside chaste in her father-in-law's house, she may adopt this course; but such instances are very rare, particularly in the case of young females, and are not to be looked for in a society, and amongst tribes, notorious for the laxity of their morals and for the degeneracy of their conceptions.

In default of surviving brothers, and in accordance with acknowledged usage, the widow is at the disposal of her father-in-law's family: From the moment she has quitted the paternal roof, she is considered to have been assigned as the property of another, and ceases to have a free will. Where the Hymeneal bond is so loosely and irrationally knit, it is not a matter of surprise, that the feeble tie and servile obligation, which unite the wife

† Intermarriages between the Jât Sikh Chiefs, and the Aloowaleah and Ramgurheah families, do not obtain, the latter being *Kulals* and *Thokas* (mace bearers and carpenters) and deemed inferior.

‡ The present Rajah of Nabah, JUSWUNT SINGH, and six of the Singh-Pooreah Chiefs, are by a connubial union of this nature. Maha Raja RUNJEET SINGH has gone some steps further: He took by *Kurawah* a lady betrothed to his father MAHA SINGH: He has also taken DYA KOONWUR and RUTUN KOONWUR, the widows of SAHEB SINGH, the chief of Goojrat, his own uncle-in-law.

to the husband, should make but an insincere and heartless impression. Females are daily accused before Chiefs and their officers of breaches of conjugal virtue, and of having absconded to evade the claims of a father, or mother-in-law, or the established rights of a Jeth, or a *Daiwur*. When they have fled into the territory of another Chief, it is often difficult to obtain their restitution, but the solicitations of a Punchayt, and the more forcible argument of reprisals, are in the end efficacious, and the unfortunate woman, if she do not in a fit of desperation take opium, or cast herself into a well, is necessitated to submit to the law of the land, which she will again violate on the first opportune occasion. Sense of shame, or feelings of honor, have no place in the breast of a Jât,* and the same may be said of men of other low tribes. They will make strenuous exertions for recovery of their wives, after they have absconded, and will take them back as often as they can get them, bickering even for the children the woman may have had by her paramour, as some recompense for her temporary absence, and for the expense and trouble they have incurred in the search for her†

Debtors and revenue defaulters who abscond, and find protection in a foreign state, are seldom demanded, and if demanded, never surrendered by even the most petty Chief. The promise is made, that, when the delinquent has the means, he shall discharge whatever sum may appear, on a scrutiny into his accounts, to be fairly due

* The old Chief Tara Singh Ghyba often declared, that a Jât's nose reached to Mooltan, and that if he lost a part of it for any offence, there would still be enough remaining. Implying that he was a stranger to shame and could survive disgrace.

† Law of Moses, Deuteronomy, Chap. 23d v. 15 and 16.

by him. It is not uncommon for a deputation, composed of the heads, or of some respectable inhabitants of a town or village, from which a person has removed, to proceed and wait upon the Chief with whom a fugitive may find an asylum, and, entering into stipulations for his personal safety, to receive him back, if he be willing to return.

In the Sikh states there are no compulsory laws for raising money for the relief of the indigent. Most fuqeers belong to a *punth* or sect, and each sect has its temples, which are endowed with lands and villages, (termed *Oordoo* and *Poora*) by the chiefs, and to which *Churhawa*, or offerings of grain and money, are made by its votaries. An elemosynary establishment is sometimes founded, in places of great resort, by chiefs and wealthy natives, and named *Suda-birt*, at which every stranger is entertained for a certain number of days, and fed gratis. Every Hindoo temple has its *Muhunt*, or head, to whom are attached his immediate *Chelas* or followers, who parade the country, towns, and villages, asking, or demanding charity, which forms the support of their superior and themselves, and is freely distributed to the needy stranger and weary traveller, who may stop at their gate, or desire a lodging and a meal within the courts of the *Thakoor-Dwara*.

The Moosulman classes have their *Peerzadas*, who make their rounds amongst their *mooreeds*, or disciples, and receive from them such *neeaz*, or offerings, as they can afford, or may choose to present. Since the decline of the Muhomedan, and the rise and establishment of the Sikh power, the *Peerzadas* have to lament the loss in many instances, and the diminution in others, of their village endowments. They still retain, however, a portion of the lands they held during the reigns of the Emperors of Delhi, attached to their principal *rozas*, tombs, or seminaries, but the rents from them, and the trifle given in *neeaz*, are barely sufficient to maintain themselves and families in respectable circumstances, and to support the *Khadims*, or servitors, in constant attendance at the tombs of their saints.

Every village, independent of the fixed dues to the blacksmith, carpenter, washerman, to choomars, and sweepers, has its *mulha*, or incidental expenses, charged on its cultivators for what are termed *aya, gya*, or grain, ghee, &c. given to wandering *fuqeers* and needy passengers. The *punch* or heads of the villages, who supply the *mulha*, collect it in cash from the villagers, twice during the year, and it not unfrequently gives rise to altercation and dispute, from the real or supposed inclination of the *punch* to impose upon them, under the specious and pious name of charity, much of which finds its way into the collectors own pocket.

Hindoo and Moosulman *fuqeers* are found located in and around every town and village, and each has his *Tukeeah*, or place of abode, to which a few beegahs of land are assigned, the gift of the Zumeendars, who, in other respects, also, take care of the common holy fraternity, that their blessing may continue to be upon them.

The *Jinsee*, or grain lands, are cessed by the *Kun*, (appraisement), or the *Butaee*, (division of the produce in the field;) both are exceptionable. It requires a very discerning and experienced man, to estimate the quantity in a field of standing grain: In some it is over, and in others under rated. The Butaee is detailed and tedious, an establishment also is required to watch the different *Kulwarah*, or heaps of grain on the field. Cultivators are apt to steal it during the night, and in stormy and wet weather much of it is damaged, ere it can be housed. It is a common saying "*Butaee lootaee*," or Butaee is plunder. Some Chiefs exact a half of the produce, others two-fifths, and a few, one-fourth. Sugar-cane, cotton, poppy, indigo, and all the lands under the denomination of the *Zubtee*, are assessed at fixed rates, and the rent is received in cash.

In the Sikh states, the lands of most towns and villages are parcelled out into puttees, turufs, or divisions, amongst the Punch, or Zumeendars, who are answerable for the *Sirkar's* or Ruler's share. In some, where there are no ostensible heads, the lands are held by *hulsaree*, or ploughs. Thus, if in a village society, there be twenty-five ploughs, and 2500 beegahs, the Jinsee and Zubtee lands, are equalized amongst the *Asamees*, or husbandmen, which gives 100 beegahs to each plough, and each Asamee pays his own rent, much on the principle of a Ryotwar settlement. In general, the Punch hold a few beegahs, and also the *Puchotrah*, (5 per cent.) on the net collections, in Inaum.

The system of assessment by the Kun or Butaee, pleases the agricultural community, and the Chiefs, who pay their armed retainers and establishments every six months in kind, with a small sum in cash called *poshakee* or clothing: it also accords with their internal plan of management. On some small estates, with comparatively few followers, it works well, but it is not at all adapted to extended territory and great governments.*

The chief sources of oppression on the people, under Sikh rule, emanate, 1st, from the exaction of the *Siwaee-Juma*, or extraordinary imposts, levied in cash on every village under the general head of the *Huq-Huboobnuzur-bhét*, and branching out into a variety of names. 2nd, The inhuman practice of *Kar-begar*, or the impress of labour of the inhabitants without recompense; and 3rd, the violence to which they are exposed from licentious armed dependents, quartered in the forts and towers which cover the country, and prey on the villages.

Every major and minor chief exercises the privilege by prescription of taxing trade, yet the duties, though levied at every ten to twenty miles, are light. A practice called *hoonda-bara* prevails in the mercantile community. A trader gives over charge of his caravan of goods to a *nanukpootrah,* who engages to convey it for a stipulated sum from Jughadree to Umritsur, the emporium of the Sikh states, paying all the duties. The *nanukpootrahs*, from the sanctity which attaches to their persons as the descendants of NANUK, the founder of the Sikh faith, enjoy certain exemptions, and are less subject to molestation from custom house importunity than others. *Beema*, or insurance, may be had at a cheap rate from the Nouhureeah merchants to all parts of India. Should any grievous or vexatious tax be imposed on

* RUNJEET SINGH, when urged by his officers to abandon the farming system, and introduce the Kun and Butaee, always replies, "that he cannot give his time and attention to the weighing and housing of grain."

the trade by a chief, he suffers an alienation of this branch of his revenue, by the route being changed through the possessions of another, who has the power to protect, and the inclination to encourage the transit of traffic through his domains.*

Sikh women do not burn with the corpse of their husbands. A single exception occurred in 1805, in the town of Booreeah, on the death of the chief RAE SINGH, when his widow made a voluntary sacrifice of herself, rejecting a handsome provision in land. There exists no prohibition against the Suttee. In all cases they are understood to be willing victims, and much real or pretended dissuasion is exercised by the public functionaries, and by friends and relations, to divert the miserable creature from her destructive intentions. That affection and duty have not always place in this class of *felo de se*, which would explain and extenuate such a deed, and convert the offspring of superstition into a noble act of self-devotion, is obvious from the frequency of Suttee, and from the fact that it is not only the favored wife, but a whole host of females, that sometimes are offered up to blaze on the pyre of their deceased lord.†

In most cases of Suttee, it will generally be observed, that a slow reluctant promise has been exacted from, or

* RUNJEET SINGH became anxious to establish a Copper Mint at Umritsur, and prohibited the importation of pice from Jughadree. The merchants of Jughadree retaliated, and withheld the exportation of copper from their town, and gained their point.

The Rajah of Puteeala has attempted to raise the duties in trade, and failed, from his territory being avoided.

† This allusion is made to the frightful scenes, which occurred on the demise of the Hill Rajahs of Kooloo, Nahun, and Juswoul, and other places.

made by the wretched woman in an unguarded moment, when under the impulse of grief. A multitude is immediately assembled round her dwelling and person; clamour and precipitancy succeed, no time is permitted for reflection; honor, shame, and duty all now combine to strengthen her bloody resolution, and the scene is hurried through and closed.*

* In 1826, after the domain of Umbala lapsed to the Hon'ble Company, a very young Brahmin woman heard of the demise of her husband in a foreign land and expressed a determination to immolate herself with part of his clothes. A concourse of people instantly gathered around her and the utmost excitation prevailed. Being absent at the time, the office Moonshee, the Thanadar of Umbala, and the Soobadar on duty, all three Hindoos of high caste, took upon themselves the task and responsibility of preventing the sacrifice, dispersed the multitude, and induced the young creature to await a reply to the express they had despatched to me. A threat to confine and prosecute all instigators, and a pension of three rupees per month saved the Brahminee, and she survives, honored in her family and respected in society as a living Suttee, totally falsifying the current belief, that recantation brings disgrace, scorn, and contempt. On the demise of the Hill Rajas of Bulaspoor and Nahun in 1824 and 1827 there was no Suttee, and the practice has disappeared in the Hill States under the protection of British Government.

NOTES.

Page 2—Last line of the page.

Initiation by drinking of the *Pahul* is a rite established by GOOROO GOVIND, and is thus described by KHOOSHWUQT RAEE. The candidate and the initiator wash their feet with water, and then put sugar into the liquid and stir it with a knife, while they repeat five quatrains, the first of which runs as follows:

Sùrawuk sidh sumoh sidhanuk dekh phiryo ghur Jogee Jutee Kee,
Soor surawuk sidh surawuk sunt sumoh unèk mutee kee—
Sare hee dēsko dekh phiryo mut kooo nu dekhut pranputee kee
Sree Bhugwan kee Bhuye kripa bin ek rutee bin ek rutee kee.

I have been round and have seen all kinds of devotees, Jogees and Jutees,
Holy men, practisers of austerities, men wrapped up in contemplation of the Divinity with all their many ways and habits,
Every country have I travelled over, but the truly godly I have seen no where,
Without the grace of God, friend, Man's lot weighs not the lowest fraction.

The other quatrains are very nearly to the same effect, we add the whole in the original character for the benefit of the curious, but do not think it worth while to translate the remainder.

सरावकसिद्ध समोहसिद्धांक देखफिरियोघर जोगीजतीके।
सूरसरावक सिद्धसरावक सन्तसमोह अनेकमतीके॥
सारेहीदेसको देखफिरयोमत् कोऊनदेखत् प्रानपतीके।
श्रीभगवानकी भाईकृपाविन ऐकरतीविन ऐकरतीके॥

माते मतंग जडे जरसंग अनूपउमंग सुरंग सुवारे।
कोटतरंग कुरंगसे कूदत् पवनको गवन को जातनिवारे॥
भारी भुजानके भूपभलो वद्ध नियावत सीस न जात विचारे।
ईतेभयेतो कहा भयेभूपत अंतको नांगेहि पावें पधारे॥

जीत फिरे सब देस दैसांको बाजत ढोलमृदंग नगारे।
गजपतको व्ह गजानके सुंदर हंसत हैं रथराज हजारे॥
भूत भविख भुवानके भूपत कौन गने नहीं जात विचारे।
ईतेभये तो कहा भये भूपत अंतको नांगेहि पायें पधारे॥

तीरथ थान दयादम दान संजमनेम अनेक विसेखे।
वेदपुरान कितावकुरान जमीनओजमान सभानके पेखे॥
पवनअहार जतीजटधार सबहीशुभचार विचारकेदेखे।
श्रीभगवंत भजे विन् भूपत एकरतो विनएक न: लेखे॥

सुद्धसिपाह दुरंत दुर्वाह सुसाज सेनाह दुर्जान दलेंगे।
भारीगुमान भरे मनमें गिरपरवत पेख हिलैं न हिलेंगे॥
तोरअरीं मरोर मवासन् माते गजानके मान मलेंगे।
श्रीभगवान कृपातुमहरी विन त्यागजहान निदान चलेंगे॥

Between each quatrain the breath is exhaled with a puff, and the beverage of mixed sugar and dirty water stirred as above, is then drunk to the toast of "*wah! wah! Govind Sikh! ap hee gooroo chela.*" Hail! hail! Govind Sikh! himself preceptor and pupil." The neophyte, after this ceremony, is a Sikh complete. It is said that when GOOROO GOVIND had only five followers, he went through this form with them, drinking of the water which had washed their feet, and they drinking that which had washed his.

Page 27—Third line from the bottom.

UMUR SINGH, of Puteeala, was the son of SURDOL SINGH, who survived his father ALA SINGH, two or three years, according to KHOOSHWUQT RAEE. When UMUR SINGH waited on AHMED SHAH, he was ordered to shave his head and beard before entering the Royal presence. By a *Nuzurana* (or present) of a lakh of rupees, he purchased permission to appear bearded and unshorn. KHOOSHWUQT RAEE says the title of Muhindur was obtained from SHAH ALUM in the time of SAHEB SINGH, and the style Muha-Raja Rajugan Buhadur was that conferred on UMUR SINGH by AHMED SHAH.

Page 39—End of the paragraph.

KHOOSHWUQT RAEE gives the same account of the death of CHURUT SINGH, which he says happened at Oodhoo-Chuk, on the Busuntur, after the two armies had been for six months encamped on opposite sides of the stream, skirmishing with one another. K. R. also confirms the story of the assassination of JHUNDA SINGH, but says he was riding about at the time with two or three orderlies. He gives the same date for these events as Captain MURRAY.

Page 40—Last line.

KHOOSHWUQT RAEE says that GUNDA SINGH, head of the Bhungee Misul, being applied to by DHURUM SINGH for aid against MAHA SINGH, made answer "Why should I destroy this youth and make over his inheritance to a servant?"

Page 41—Eighth line from the bottom.

KHOOSHWUQT RAEE says the *Bhungee Top* had been taken by CHURUT SINGH from LEHNA SINGH, but the carriage breaking down in the attempt to carry it to Gujraolee, it was left in deposit with the Zumeendars of Rusool Nugur, until it should be re-demanded by the captor. The restoration of the gun to the Bhungees was therefore a breach of faith.

Page 43—Ninth line from the bottom.

KHOOSHWUQT RAEE names several families which had found refuge in Jummoo, during the troubles of the Punjab.

Amongst others, MULIKA ZUMANEE, a Dehlee Queen, and one of the widows of MEER MUNOO. HUREE SINGH, the son with other members of the family of Raja KAONRA MUL, was also living there in splendour; and DILPUT RAEE, the son of LUKHPUT RAEE, had likewise settled there, with the remains of several other families of Nobles of the Dehlee, or Vice Regal Courts. RUNJEET DEO treated all these refugees with much distinction, and particularly enjoined his son to continue to them the same courtesy. BRIJ RAJ, however, was no sooner seated on the Gudee, than he made them the objects of his extortion. From HUREE SINGH he is said to have obtained 50 lakhs of rupees.

Page 43—End of the second paragraph.

KHOOSHWUQT RAEE states the plunder obtained by MAHA SINGH, from Jummoo, at two Krores of Rupees, but this seems much exaggerated. He also states that BRIJ RAJ had been killed in an action with a Bhungee detachment, and his son, CHYT SINGH, was the Raja, when MAHA SINGH captured and sacked the town.

Page 44—14th line from the bottom.

According to K. R., JY SINGH ordered his people to shoot MAHA SINGH, and GOOR BUKHSH, his son, in vain interceded to save him,—he also says, that MAHA SINGH went off immediately from the interview, and was pursued and fired at as far as the village of Mejithia, but escaped fortunately without injury,

Page 49—End.

KHOOSHWUQT RAEE is silent in respect to the fate of RUNJEET SINGH'S Mother, but admits that the Dewan was made away with, and adds that RUNJEET was for some time after distrustful of the whole race of Mootusudees, and would employ none.

Page 53—End of the page.

JUSA SINGH of Chunduneeot, or Cheniot, is said to have surrendered to RUNJEET SINGH, upon a promise of restoration sworn on the Holy Grunth, but was nevertheless made prisoner immediately on presenting himself, and stripped of all his possessions. RUNJEET SINGH being taxed with the perjury, called for the holy volumes on which he had sworn, and the wrappers being opened, some bricks in the shape of books were all that was found.

Page 54—End of the paragraph.

GOOLAB SINGH Bhungee died, it is said, from excessive drinking. Lohgurh stood a siege, and was taken by assault,—the besiegers having found entrance by a wicket gate, left open to act as an embrasure for an enormous gun. The place was taken in the midst of a storm in the month of December, and GOORDUT and his mother escaping, were all night exposed to the cold and rain, but found refuge at last with JODH SINGH, head of the Rumgurheea Misul, whose fort Ramgurh was not very far distant. RUNJEET SINGH found his aunt, the sister of MAHA SINGH, in the fort, and sent her off in a *ruth*, or covered cart, next morning, to share the misfortunes of RANEE SOOKHA.

Page 60—End of the paragraph.

The result of RUNJEET SINGH's expedition of this season, from the time of his leaving Umritsur until his return, is stated by KHOOSHWUQT RAEE, to have been seven elephants, nine pieces of ordnance, fifty horses, and about two lakhs of rupees in cash.

Page 60—Also.

In 1807, JODH SINGH was gained over to close alliance with RUNJEET, and K. R. gives a long detail of the means used to cajole him. Amongst other things, RUNJEET SINGH asked permission to inspect the fort of Ramgurh, and went there thinly attended. He professed great admiration of the fortifications, and ordered the foundations of a fort for himself, afterwards called Govindgurh, to be laid down according to the same plan. JODH SINGH was the son of JUSA SINGH, MAHA SINGH's ally against JY SINGH. He joined with his Misul the army that was led by RUNJEET SINGH against Kasoor in 1807, which is stated at 30,000 horse, being the united force of the Sookurchukeeas, Ghuneeas, Aloowalas, and Rumgurheeas. After eight days' fighting, an out-work of the place was carried, when SHURF-OOD-DEEN and others deserting, KOOTUB-OOD-DEEN surrendered.

Page 61—Tenth line.

MOZUFFUR KHAN is said to have paid eighty thousand rupees, and to have given five horses to be rid of the Sikh army. During the march back, a Zumeendar came up mounted on a fine horse to pay his respects. RUNJEET SINGH coveted the horse, and his over zealous courtiers demanded it rudely. The rider being offended, rode up to RUNJEET'S elephant and made several cuts at him. The guard and attendants gathered round, but none was found that could match the Zumeendar in horsemanship and sword-play. After having wounded and unhorsed several, he was shot and his horse thus secured.

Page 63—Eleventh line.

It was about this time, that is, towards the close of 1807, that MOHKUM CHUND presented himself at the Court of RUNJEET SINGH, and was appointed Dewan. He had served in this capacity with SAHEB SINGH of Goojrat, and, until his appointment, RUNJEET SINGH had no officer of this description.

Page 63—The end.

K. R. assigns the capture of Puthan Kot and Seeal Kot to the previous season, that is, 1807-8.

Page 68—Middle of the page.

KHOOSHWUQT RAEE says the Akalees intended to have taken their revenge upon the mission by a night attack, to prevent which RUNJEET SINGH sent 500 of his best troops to mount guard about Sir CHARLES METCALFE's camp. In the morning, Sir CHARLES moved to a greater distance from Umritsur, and the Akalees dug up and burned the buried biers and every relic they could find of the Mohumedan rite.

Page 77—Middle of the page.

SUNSAR CHUND played a double part through the whole of this negociation. After his engagement with RUNJEET SINGH, he entered into treaty with UMUR SINGH, promising to surrender the fort to him, and thus obtaining leave to bring away his family, contrived to throw into the place his brother with four months supplies, thus hoping to keep it against both claimants. RUNJEET SINGH, however, seized UNRODH CHUND as a hostage, and obtaining from SUNSAR CHUND an order to be received into the place, bribed UMUR SINGH, whose army was sickly and pressed for supplies, in order to secure access to the gate, when no opposition was offered to his entrance.

Page 78—Last line.

K. R. says that upon GOOLAB SINGH's flying to RUNJEET's camp, SAHEB SINGH of Goojrat, the father, took fright and fled to Bhimbur, whereupon his whole territory, and the treasure and property in his forts, were quickly taken possession of by RUNJEET, and a Jageer of 12,000 Rs. per annum was assigned to GOOLAB SINGH. The plunder of this family is stated to have yielded between five and six lakhs of rupees in cash and seven hundred villages. In 1810, SAHEB SINGH gave himself up and obtained a Jageer of rupees 25,000 per annum.

Page 79—Fourth line from the bottom.

According to KHOOSHWUQT RAEE, SHAH SHOOJA was invited to Mooltan by MOOZUFFUR KHAN, with whom VUFA BEGUM, with the Shah's family, had already taken refuge, and had brought the Shah's jewels. MOOZUFFUR KHAN declared, he required the Shah's aid and countenance to enable him to withstand the attacks of RUNJEET SINGH. He no sooner, however, made his appearance under the walls, than the fort guns were opened on him, from which K. R. surmises that the Kiladar wished the death of the Shah, in order that he might plunder the jewels, or if he surrendered, that it was his intention to have given him up to Prince KAMRAN, which would equally have answered his purpose. SHAH SHOOJA rode away beyond the reach of the fort guns, but remained in the neighbourhood until MOOZUFFUR KHAN repenting, assigned over four Purgunas, with a Jageer of 10,000, for the Shah's personal expences.

Page 153—Tenth line from the bottom.

And page 170.

ABBAS MEERZA died in the early part of the present year 1834. It must be recollected, however, that this work was compiled and prepared for publication in 1833. The argument holds, whoever may be the competitor for the Persian Throne, whose cause may be espoused by the Russian Autocrat. The party at the Court of Tehran, who look to that quarter, will not have been extinguished by the death of the individual Prince, whose name was to the contract entered into.

INDEX OF PRINCIPAL PERSONS.

A.

B.

K.

L.

M.

N.

S.

T.

U.

V.

W.

Y.

Z.

THE END.